Performance and Migration

T0371776

This third volume in the 4x45 series addresses some of the most current and urgent performance work in contemporary theatre practice. As people from all backgrounds and cultures criss-cross the globe with an ever-growing series of pushes and pulls guiding their movements, this book explores contemporary artists who have responded to various forms of migration in their theatre, performance and multimedia work.

The volume comprises two lectures and two curated conversations with theatre-makers and artists. Danish scholar of contemporary visual culture, Anne Ring Petersen, brings artistic and political aspects of 'postmigration' to the fore in an essay on the innovations of Shermin Langhoff at Berlin's Ballhaus Naunynstraße, and the decolonial work of Danish-Trinidadian artist Jeannette Ehlers. The racialised and gendered exclusions associated with navigating 'the industry' for non-white female and non-white non-binary artists are interrogated in Melbourne-based theatre scholar Paul Rae's interview with two Australian performers of Indian heritage, Sonya Suares and Raina Peterson. UK playwrights Joe Murphy and Joe Robertson of Good Chance Theatre discuss their work in dialogue, and with their colleague, Iranian animator and illustrator Majid Adin. Emma Cox's essay on Irish artist Richard Mosse's video installation, *Incoming*, discusses thermographic 'heat signatures' as means of seeing migrants and the imperative of envisioning global climate change.

An accessible and forward-thinking exploration of one of contemporary performance's most pressing influences, 4x45 | *Performance and Migration* is a unique resource for scholars, students and practitioners of Theatre Studies, Performance Studies and Human Geography.

Emma Cox is a Reader in the Department of Drama, Theatre and Dance at Royal Holloway, University of London.

4x45
Series Editor – Andy Lavender

The *4x45* project introduces a new series of short video lectures from Digital Theatre+ accompanied by transcript books, addressing key topics and emerging debates in theatre and performance.

Each entry in the series comprises four lectures, interviews and discussions from theatre experts, based around common themes and presented as 45-minute videos hosted on the Digital Theatre+ website. The edited companion books contain a link to this multimedia component and four written transcripts of the videos with related discussions.

4x45 talks aim to respond quickly to emerging issues and developments in all aspects of theatre and performance, reflecting and defining the important conversations across the field.

The Theatre of Katie Mitchell
Edited by Benjamin Fowler

Neoliberalism, Theatre and Performance
Edited by Andy Lavender

Performance and Migration
Edited by Emma Cox

For more information about this series, please visit: https://www.routledge.com/4x45/book-series/4x45

Performance and Migration

Edited by Emma Cox

Routledge
Taylor & Francis Group

LONDON AND NEW YORK

First published 2022
by Routledge
2 Park Square, Milton Park, Abingdon, Oxon OX14 4RN

and by Routledge
605 Third Avenue, New York, NY 10158

Routledge is an imprint of the Taylor & Francis Group, an informa business

British Library Cataloguing-in-Publication Data
A catalogue record for this book is available from the British Library

Library of Congress Cataloging-in-Publication Data
Names: Cox, Emma, editor.
Title: Performance and migration / edited by Emma Cox.
Description: Abingdon, Oxon; New York: Taylor and Francis, 2022. |
Series: 4x45 series | Includes bibliographical references.
Identifiers: LCCN 2021014235 (print) | LCCN 2021014236 (ebook) |
ISBN 9781032058962 (paperback) | ISBN 9781032059037 (hardback) |
ISBN 9781003199755 (ebook)
Subjects: LCSH: Arts and society. | Theater and society. | Emigration and immigration in art. | Performing arts—Themes, motives.
Classification: LCC NX180.S6 P4435 2022 (print) | LCC NX180.S6 (ebook) | DDC 700.1/03—dc23
LC record available at https://lccn.loc.gov/2021014235
LC ebook record available at https://lccn.loc.gov/2021014236

ISBN: 978-1-032-05903-7 (hbk)
ISBN: 978-1-032-05896-2 (pbk)
ISBN: 978-1-003-19975-5 (ebk)

DOI: 10.4324/9781003199755

Typeset in Bembo
by codeMantra

Contents

Contributors

Majid Adin is an artist and animator from Iran, now living in the UK. In 2017 he won a competition to produce an animated music video for Elton John's 'Rocket Man'. His graphic novel, *Hamid and Shakespeare*, was published in 2021.

Emma Cox is a Reader in Drama and Theatre at Royal Holloway, University of London. She is the author of *Performing Noncitizenship* (2015) and *Theatre & Migration* (2014), editor of *Staging Asylum* (2013) and co-editor of *Refugee Imaginaries: Research Across the Humanities* (2020).

Joe Murphy and Joe Robertson are co-Artistic Directors of Good Chance, which they founded at the Calais Jungle in 2015. Good Chance build temporary arts spaces in large geodesic domes in areas with high refugee populations. Their play, *The Jungle*, a co-production with the National Theatre and Young Vic, premiered in London in 2017 and was staged in New York in 2018.

Anne Ring Petersen is a Professor in the Department of Arts and Cultural Studies at the University of Copenhagen. Her research explores transcultural and migratory approaches to art and cultural production. Her current research project, 'Togetherness in Difference: Reimagining Identities, Communities and Histories through Art' (2019–2023), develops topics from *Migration into Art: Transcultural Identities and Art-Making in a Globalised World* (2017) and the co-authored book *Reframing Migration, Diversity and the Arts: The Postmigrant Condition* (2019).

Raina Peterson is a Melbourne-based choreographer and dancer. They teach and practice the South Indian classical dance form of Mohiniyattam, and make experimental dance and queer cabaret with their company, Karma Dance.

Paul Rae is an Associate Professor of Theatre Studies and Head of the School of Culture and Communication at the University of Melbourne. He is the author of *Theatre & Human Rights* (2009), and *Real Theatre: Essays in Experience* (2019).

Sonya Suares is an Australian multidisciplinary performer, dramaturg, director, producer and arts activist. She is founder of the award-winning theatre company Watch This and works widely across television and mainstream and independent theatre.

Introduction
Performance and migration

Emma Cox

The current century's frenetically mobile character has been shown by a novel human virus to be a vulnerable set of conditions, and not – as many might reasonably have assumed – an economic, technological and social inevitability. The publication of this volume of Digital Theatre's 4x45 series, *Performance and Migration*, coincides with restrictions on movement and assembly that have radically curtailed the work of all of the artists named in these pages, whether they are from migrant backgrounds or not. Of course, the determination of human life in the context of power structures that shape a body's movement within and across territories, its day-to-day mobility, its taking of risk, is nothing new to some: refugees embody a legal status that depends precariously upon the nation state, even as the state is often what prohibits forced migration by administrating it as 'unauthorised' or 'illegal'. Rather than as any sort of leveller, therefore, it seems more useful to perceive the Covid-19 pandemic as bringing into a wider field of vision the privileges and hardships that already shape the means by which people migrate, and the means by which art is made in migration's wake. This issue includes discussions of artistic works that were

DOI: 10.4324/9781003199755

made during and in response to a pre-pandemic crisis, the so-called 'migrant crisis' in Europe of 2015–2016, marked as it was by the arrival of large numbers of mostly Syrian refugees into the EU. If, on the one hand, our current predicament has slowed the pace of international migration to an unprecedented degree, it has also made visible – and for many, visceral – the extent to which human movement was always contingent upon the rights and freedoms assigned to categories of person by sovereign nations. Perhaps now, more than ever, a greater number of people are thinking about how migration is authorised by states, how it is experienced by individuals – and how far it underlies the capacity to imagine a future.

This volume comprises two lectures and two curated conversations with theatre-makers and artists. Danish scholar of contemporary visual culture, Anne Ring Petersen, brings artistic and political aspects of 'postmigration' to the fore in an essay on the innovations of Shermin Langhoff at Berlin's Ballhaus Naunynstraße, and the decolonial work of Danish-Trinidadian artist Jeannette Ehlers. The racialised and gendered exclusions associated with navigating 'the industry' for non-white female and non-white non-binary artists are interrogated in Melbourne-based British theatre scholar Paul Rae's interview with two Australian performers of Indian heritage, Sonya Suares and Raina Peterson. The representation and participation of refugees in arts projects is a central focus of an interview with playwrights Joe Murphy and Joe Robertson of London-based Good Chance Theatre, part of which includes a conversation with Iranian animator and illustrator Majid Adin. Thermographic 'heat signatures' as a means of seeing migrants are linked with the imperative of envisioning global climate change in my own (London-based New Zealand theatre scholar Emma Cox) essay on

Irish artist Richard Mosse's video installation, *Incoming*. The four videos that accompany this text were filmed in the UK, Denmark and Australia during 2018–2020. They offer a range of perspectives on the vast topic of performance and migration, moving from refugee art-making collectives in fringe territories of France, to mainstage drama in the UK, to a piece of videography encompassing images from the Persian Gulf to the Saharan desert to the borders of Europe, to anti-racist performance art shown in Germany, the US, the UK and Denmark, to queer classical Indian inflected dance performance in Australia. While this range must necessarily be selective, it is hoped that the artistic forms, the modes of collaboration, the provocations and the cultural contexts introduced here will generate points of connection for readers seeking to approach elsewhere the rich, confounding, messy nexus of performance and migration.

Artistic and cultural contexts within Germany and Denmark inform Anne Ring Petersen's discussion in her essay, 'Migratory Aesthetics and Postmigrant Performance', the first contribution to this volume. A core idea in Petersen's piece is specific to continental (mostly northern) European discourses on migration: the *postmigrant*. This term is largely unfamiliar in Anglophone contexts but has gained traction in Europe as a means by which theorists and artists have, as Petersen puts it, considered 'the social and cultural processes and struggles that come *after* migration', with the temporality of this 'after' understood as intergenerational. The idea of postmigrancy frames an interest in the multicultural or multiethnic societies that emerge after demographic changes, and is attentive to the structural bases of those changes. Crucially, however, postmigration opens up, as Petersen explains, a '*process* of questioning and reinvention' that is not limited to descendants of migrants.

In the European sphere, Petersen identifies a belated cultural 'realisation that European societies have been profoundly changed by postcolonial and labour migration into Europe after the Second World War'. The 'postcolonial' (a term whose prefix 'post' signals a continued contestation-with, rather than an afterwards) is inflected differently in Europe than in former settler-colonies such as Australia, whose reckonings with the past are substantially oriented towards violence against indigenous populations, and whose multiculturalism is underpinned by the prioritisation (once explicit, and latterly invisibilised) of the majority white population.

Petersen seeks to pinpoint why the concept of postmigration resonates in European societies, particularly Germany, but not in settler-colonial nations such as Australia:

> In German social sciences and cultural studies, the concept of *das Postmigrantische* – or, in English, 'the postmigratory' or 'postmigration' - has been introduced as an explanatory framework that captures the conflictual dynamics of globalised societies such as European societies. They differ from multicultural 'immigrant nations' such as the US, Canada and Australia in that immigration is not central to their national self-perceptions but in many cases perceived as a threat to national identity and culture. Consequently, even descendants of migrants can be perceived as racialised 'Others', as those who do not truly belong to the imagined community of the nation.
>
> (15)

The distinction is a useful one in its identification of immigrant nations as those in which migration is 'central to […] national self-perceptions'. At the same time, it is important to remember that so-called 'immigrant nations' are also settler-colonial nations whose histories of arrival map on to the imperialist paradigms that founded them.

As Paul Rae reminds us in the curated artist dialogue, 'Being Second Generation', which comprises the second contribution to this issue, colonial era tensions and the violence of Pacific Islander labour migration entrenched 'attitudes' in what would become the nation of Australia that 'set the tone of things to come' (35). Rae explains: 'Australia was federated into a single nation state in 1901, and introduced the Immigration Restriction Act, better known as the "White Australia Policy", which would not be conclusively abolished until 1973' (35). Rae opens up a conversation with Melbourne-based, Indian Australian artists, Sonya Suares and Raina Peterson, which shows that 'being second generation' is directly about negotiating self- and externally perceived otherness. In Suares and Peterson's discussion it becomes clear that the character of this otherness derives from a fundamentally racist imagined community, where different contingents of migrant-descended people have different experiences in terms of day-to-day life, and in terms of navigating the performing arts as a profession.

Similarities and differences between the term *postmigrant* and the term *second generation*, the latter framing Rae's interview with Suares and Peterson, are inevitably considered as a result of their juxtaposition in this volume. Anne Ring Petersen's suggestion that in the European sphere the concept of postmigration goes some way towards addressing the tendency in state-driven constructions of multiculturalism towards 'ethnic labelling' sits uneasily alongside Suares and Peterson's responses to life-long experiences of racism. Suares recalls being repeatedly asked by another child at primary school, 'Sonya have you decided whether you're Indian or Australian?' (42), a circular interrogation that morphed into an existential dilemma for Suares. This is a clear illustration of the extent to which white Australian ethnicity stands as the invisible norm within the nation, despite various attempts over several decades in both policy and non-governmental arenas to open up this ethno-cultural monolith. The notion that Australianness and Indian-Australianness are separate categories persists, and Suares and Peterson's discussion seems to suggest that instead of moving away from ethnic label-ling (and relatedly, from performing arts practices explicitly rooted in Indianness), the Australian arts industry, and wider culture, needs to talk *more* and in *more direct terms* about race.

In 'Good Chance Theatre: Margins and Main Stages', a conversation between Joe Murphy and Joe Robertson, co-artistic directors of Good Chance Theatre, insights emerge into the kind of multicultural spaces the pair en-countered, as well as those they actively forged, when they travelled to the notorious Jungle refugee encampment at Calais, France, in 2015, the year before its demolition by French authorities in 2016. Murphy and Robertson's suc-cessful play *The Jungle*, which premiered at the Young Vic in London before its West End and Broadway transfers in 2018, exists as a document and testament of sorts to this pe-riod of time. While Murphy and Robertson's play – which is among the most high-profile works on the topic – is an important part of the discussion, what is also offered here is an insight into the complex social dynamics of the Calais period from its earliest days, oriented in and around the 'dome', the arts space Murphy and Robertson constructed at the camp. In the febrile, transient environment of the Jungle, the need to share and exchange life stories was,

Robertson recalls, immediately 'palpable' – as he explains: 'we'd shake their hands and before you'd even found out their name you were hearing about what was happening, and where that person had come from, and in that atmosphere, I think that was very interesting for us as playwrights' (62). Privation and creative energy co-existed in a way that confounded expectations for the pair of British visitors to this unhomely home for refugees.

Murphy and Robertson use the name 'Good Chance' to refer to the company that 'builds the theatres': that is, they understand the endeavour of constructing domes as collectivist arts spaces – in Calais and later Paris – as being at the heart of what they do, whereas the staging of *The Jungle* in professional theatrical venues of London's Young Vic and the Playhouse Theatre represents *partnerships*. This oscillation between a somewhat purist sensibility and a savvy instinct for professional compromise characterises Murphy and Robertson's unique position as figures whose work moves between sites of cultural production, adapting to the priorities (both artistic and economic) of professionalisation and non-professionalisation. A distinction takes shape in Murphy and Robertson's conversation between 'theatre' as a gathering, an assembly, alive to the contingencies of the unfolding moment and to a range of unpredictable interpersonal encounters, versus 'theatre' as an event framed by the conventions of ticketing and fixed seating. As Murphy puts it, the latter is structured in such a way that audiences are implicitly assured that 'all will be well', and there is a 'limit to your involvement' (63–64). Whether or not such a distinction holds up to deeper scrutiny, it is clear that, for Murphy and Robertson, the open format of creative gatherings within Good Chance's temporary domes offers greater scope for energisation, participation and, perhaps most importantly, hospitality. In this sense, the conversation as it unfolds starts to gnaw away at Murphy's own initial query over the purchase of the term *participatory*.

Part 2 of the Good Chance contribution centres on the life and work of UK-based Iranian animator and illustrator, Majid Adin, as he joins Murphy and Robertson in conversation. In 2017, Adin won a prestigious international prize to create a video for Elton John's hit *Rocket Man*. The resulting animation is a realist-futurist image-scape of loss and disorientation, where the figure of a refugee-cum-astronaut departs his homeland and travels a vast, intergalactic distance before descending and landing in an alien city – a place that is recognisable as a dystopian London. Adin became acquainted with Murphy and Robertson while he was an asylum seeker at Calais, attempting to enter the UK by one of the rare, risky routes available to would-be refugees. The trio later reconnected in London. The Digital Theatre video of their conversation conveys an interpersonal dynamic that may be less perceptible in transcript form; what the filmed dialogue demonstrates is that the aesthetic and practical dimensions of collaboration are sustained by a friendship, allyship and mutual respect that was first sparked at the Jungle in Calais.

Imagistically and thematically, Irish artist Richard Mosse's 2017 video installation *Incoming*, discussed in 'The Heat Signatures of Refugee Transit', the fourth and final contribution to this volume, shares certain affinities with Good Chance's play *The Jungle*, most explicitly in a sequence in the former of the fiery, forcible dismantling of the Calais encampment in 2016. In terms of positionality, too, critical similarities exist between *Incoming* and *The Jungle* as works created by white male artists, whose awareness of their inherent privileges both contributes to their works' complexity, and renders opaque certain lines of enquiry concerning process: the professional connections, the networks, the influence, and the freedoms of movement into and out of spaces of abjection, and into and out of spaces of high cultural capital. In Mosse's case, the extraordinary succession of images presented in *Incoming* includes footage filmed from aboard a US aircraft carrier in the Persian Gulf, close-up imagery of a migrant vessel coming ashore at Lesvos, an autopsy of a migrant, sequences filmed from a people smuggling route in the Sahara, as well as images from refugee camps in Europe. These are filmed using a high-grade thermographic camera, an instrument that is classified as weapon for the purposes of the cross-border encounters that Mosse undertook whilst making the work. Like Murphy and Robertson, then, Mosse uses tools, techniques, legal pathways and professional relationships that exemplify a privileged access to both geographical territories and cultural spaces. These men are artist-adventurers of a sort, for whom sites that would represent danger to vulnerable or oppressed bodies, and cultural spaces from which such bodies are excluded, are vanguards of artistic invention. No matter how consciously and humbly these artists undertake their work, no matter how consultative and questioning their approach, the neo-colonial structural frameworks that permit and propel their endeavours are inescapable.

Embedded in the core vocabularies of Murphy and Robertson's and Mosse's art – Good Chance and *Incoming* – is a sense of forced migration that is occupied with propulsion, with unsteady arrival (or landing) zones, and with acceleration into the future. In contrast, the social and political character of *dwelling* comes more to the fore in Anne Ring Petersen's and Paul Rae's contributions. The terminology of postmigrant and second generation signals an explicit engagement not just with legacies (in the sense of historical residues), but with *ongoing* lived effects. For Sonya Suares and Raina Peterson, being second generation means an engagement, an entanglement and sometimes a contestation. It speaks to a continual negotiation with what is present in one's life, and not simply what preceded it. Here, Christina Sharpe's concept of 'wake work', theorised in the different but not unrelated context of slavery's legacies in the present, is resonant. In her book *In the Wake: On Blackness and Being*, which positions transatlantic slavery 'as a problem of and for thought' (2016, 5), Sharpe grapples with its presence in black consciousness, writing that slavery 'was and is the disaster', its structural and personal afterlives 'deeply atemporal' (2016, 5). These observations chime with Petersen's comments on Jeanette Ehlers' *Whip it Good*, a work that, Petersen writes, 'should not be seen merely as a critique of a colonial past but also as a creative reimagination of history that inspires us to change things in the present' (27). Ehlers' piece invited audiences to participate in the central motif of flogging a white canvas, thereby to intensify investment in a reframed act of violence as 'co-actors in a performative critique of history' (27). Raina Peterson's *Third Nature*, co-created with Govind Pillai and one of the works described in dialogue with Suares, combined the classical Indian dance forms of Mohiniyattam and Bharatanatyam and featured a luxuriant set comprised of thick paper jasmine strands, the aphrodisiacal flower representing the abundance of pre-colonial South Asia. In this queering of classical Indian dance in contemporary Australian performance, the construction of a vivid, aestheticised atmosphere is a means of retracing the intergenerational threads of migration, as the past opens out like the wake of a ship.

1

Migratory aesthetics and postmigrant performance

Anne Ring Petersen

Link | https://www.digitaltheatreplus.com/education/
collections/digital-theatre/migratory-aesthetics-and-
postmigrant-performance-a-lecture-by

As early as the 1990s, sociologist Stephen Castles and polit-ical scientist Mark J. Miller (Castles and Miller [1993] 2009) proposed that we live in 'the age of migration'. This percep-tion has become widely accepted among scholars around the world. Recent global developments have infused a new sense of urgency into Castles and Miller's observation. Work-related migration and forced migration, especially as a result of on-going wars, civil conflicts and ecological crises, have probably never been more extensive than today. As a result, mass migra-tion and its consequences have become political issues of great concern. In some of the most recent studies of migration, mi-gratory movement is no longer perceived as an abnormality or exception, but rather as an integral part of society and as a naturalised part of everyday life that has influenced – and will continue to influence – most societies around the globe. In recent years, a new term has been introduced to capture this change of perception: postmigration.

DOI: 10.4324/9781003199755-1

The starting point of this lecture is debates on postmigration and culture. These primarily concern thinking and cultural production in Germany and Denmark, but they have a much wider global resonance, because they are part of the texture of response in Europe to the global migration scenario. In this lecture, I will talk about the impact of migration and postmigration on contemporary art, theatre and performance, and how issues related to migration and postcolonial critique surface in works of art and in theatre productions. In other words, I will not focus on the performing arts as an isolated field, but take an interdisciplinary approach. The ways in which issues and histories of migration are addressed in performance have many similarities with the way in which migration is reflected on in other art forms, so it makes good sense to cross the boundaries between the arts – as many practitioners do themselves. Because I take an interdisciplinary approach, my understanding of 'performance' and my use of the term must be a broad and flexible one: I will use the term to refer to specific works of performance art and to the performance of actors, as well as considering the 'performative', which is understood as the generative and participatory aspect of the spectator's interaction with the work.

Recent years have seen a significant rise in the numbers of migrants and refugees. In 2017, the United Nations estimated that there are now about 258 million transnational migrants in the world – an increase of almost 50% since 2000. The number of international migrants includes 26 million refugees and asylum seekers, or about 10% of the total (UN 2017). Due to this increasing mobility, existing challenges related to security, rights and integration will only grow and intensify in the future. Notably, receiving countries will have to deal with lasting changes and face significant political, social and cultural challenges. Recent flows of refugees and wider patterns of migration have pushed questions of integration, cultural encounters and cultural values, as well as questions of citizenship and the sharing of democratic values, to the top of the political agenda within receiving countries. The humanities – including studies in culture and the arts – can contribute significant insights, because the struggles over culture, identity, representation and (imagined) community at the core of these challenges are precisely their critical and conceptual priorities. And, importantly, these struggles are often engaged and responded to with poignancy in the arts.

It has become increasingly evident that those who study culture and the arts also need to engage with the fact that 'togetherness in difference' has become a common state of affairs (Ang 2001, 17), because this condition has also affected artistic practices and thus also works of art. To engage with cultural encounters and differences as they present themselves in works of art, we need new frameworks for understanding art. I think that postmigrant and postcolonial perspectives can provide us with some useful frameworks, so I will look at contemporary performance art and theatre from these two perspectives. The following discussion has five parts. First, I will consider the concept of postmigration and its historical origin in so-called 'postmigrant theatre'. Second, I will introduce an analytical concept that is useful in studies of art and performance: 'migratory aesthetics'. Third, I will briefly introduce my approach to postcolonial and decolonial perspectives, their similarities and differences, because these are crucial to the artist that I discuss. Fourth, I will consider a work by the

Copenhagen-based multi-media artist Jeannette Ehlers. Taking her performance *Whip It Good* from 2013 as my example, I wish to demonstrate how postmigrant and post-colonial perspectives can interact in a productive way in a performance such as this one. Finally, I will contextualise Ehlers' performance by briefly considering her first theatre production, *Into the Dark* from 2017.

The origin of the term 'postmigrant' in postmigrant theatre

In this analysis, it is not my purpose to focus directly on practices of migration, i.e. the very act of migration and the actual movements of people, nor on the ways in which these movements are represented and reflected on in the arts. Rather, I focus on the social and cultural processes and struggles that come *after* migration. In contemporary globalised societies there is a constant coming and going of people, which means that the process of cultural mixing is an ongoing one. In continental Europe, the realisation that European societies have been profoundly changed by postcolonial and labour migration into Europe after the Second World War is a recent one, and in some countries only a nascent one. Countless politicians have sought to win votes by being tough on immigration and by promising to stem the tide of refugees. At the same time, the reputation of multicultural policies has been severely tainted.

Historically, there have been two different approaches to multicultural policies. One is the assimilationist approach, which sees multicultural society as a 'melting pot'. The melting pot is a metaphor for a heterogeneous society becoming more homogeneous, as different types of people blend into one, typically according to a supposed shared 'national identity'. The other approach sees cultural diversity and difference as positive things. It is a relativist approach that perceives society as a 'salad bowl' where different cultures coexist but remain distinct in some aspects. However, this kind of multiculturalism that seeks to maintain the distinctiveness of minority ethnic communities tends to place a particular burden on cultural producers: their works are often expected to express a specific national, ethnic or religious *group* identity. As a result, stereotyped ethnic labels are often assigned to cultural producers and their work.

The postmigrant approach offers ways of sidestepping some of these challenges of multiculturalism and ethnic labelling. In German social sciences and cultural studies, the concept of *das Postmigrantische* – or, in English, 'the postmigratory' or 'postmigration' - has been introduced as an explanatory framework that captures the conflictual dynamics of globalised societies such as European ones. They differ from multicultural 'immigrant nations' such as the US, Canada and Australia in that immigration is not central to national self-perception but in many cases perceived as a threat to national identity and culture. Consequently, even descendants of migrants can be perceived as racialised 'Others', as those who do not truly belong to the imagined community of the nation.

German social scientist Naika Foroutan has called European societies 'postmigrant societies' to indicate that they are in the process of realising that 'the nation' is a culturally diverse and not a homogeneous community, and that established values, hierarchies and national self-perceptions need to be re-negotiated because of the profound changes that the pluralisation of society has brought about. Accordingly,

Foroutan et al. (2015) aptly describe postmigrant society as a 'society of negotiation'. Postmigration is thus a new concept and a new discourse that seeks to shift the perspective on migration, culture and society. Interestingly, the critical use of the term originated in artistic circles in Berlin, notably in theatre. Shermin Langhoff is often credited as the person who first introduced the term around 2004–2006. She also provided the idea with an institutional framework: in 2008, Langhoff co-founded and became the artistic director of the Ballhaus Naunynstraße theatre – a small independent theatre in the multicultural area of Kreuzberg in Berlin.

Crazy Blood: a postmigrant theatre production

In this section I use the Ballhaus Naunynstraße theatre's most successful production, *Verrücktes Blut* – in English, *Crazy Blood* – to illustrate some key ideas associated with postmigration. This play, by Nurkan Erpulat and Jens Hillje, premiered in 2011. It effectively subverts the stereotyped identities often ascribed to ethnic minorities, particularly to racialised and Islamified bodies, both in society at large and in the world of theatre and film. *Crazy Blood* has generally been received by critics and audiences as engaging debates on integration and intercultural encounters in an intelligent and humorous way (Schramm 2015, 95–98). The play is set in a contemporary German classroom. It portrays a teacher's failed attempt to teach Friedrich Schiller's play *The Robbers* from 1781 to a class of teenagers, the majority of whom have a so-called migration background. The class is chaotic, the students are disinterested and spend most of their time using their smart phones, and they swear at each other and at their teacher. Suddenly a loaded gun appears from one of the students' bags.

Instead of confiscating it, the desperate teacher Sonia uses the gun to hold the class hostage for a lesson on Schiller and the idea of aesthetic education. She forces the students to re-hearse *The Robbers* – a play that addresses questions of honour, family and individuality and is relevant to the lives of these teenagers. Gun in hand, she finally achieves her goal: to make her students perform Schiller's play and, with the help of a coercive kind of 'education', to contribute to developing their attitudes and personalities.

The irony of the plot is difficult to overlook, as the play subverts the stereotypes of disobedient youngsters from minority ethnic groups by exaggerating them. Yet, the fact that Sonia enforces this 'education' by taking the students hostage arguably calls into question Sonia's own way of practicing the 'enlightened' values that she – and the national school system – seeks to convey to students. As post-migration researcher and literary scholar Moritz Schramm has pointed out, the teacher's use of a gun to coerce students into participation reveals the underlying structures of power and coercion in education and integration. *Crazy Blood* thus suggests that education and integration are not processes of free participation, but social dynamics based on power relations and oppression (Schramm 2015, 98).

The play also puts front and centre the question of identity, particularly the interrelations between authenticity and theatrical performance in the formation of identity. In the first scene, for example, the actors arrive on stage in their ordinary clothes and begin to put on their teenage costumes – jeans, baseball-caps, sneakers. The boundary between authentic and performed identity is thus effectively blurred as they undergo the symbolic transformation into disobedient teenagers, i.e. the roles they perform, right in front of the audience and not before they go on stage.

Postmigrant theatre: institutionalisation

The Ballhaus Naunynstraße was the first theatre to actively position itself as 'postmigrant'. Since its founding in 2008, the theatre has been instrumental in bringing the idea of post-migration into the public realm (Stewart 2017, 56). It is important to stress that the term was introduced as a self-chosen descriptor. Lizzie Stewart, a scholar of theatre and migration studies, has noted that the success of the Ballhaus theatre's productions and self-labelling strategy has made the term postmigrant emerge as one of the potential alternatives to the sociological categorisation of 'people with a migration background'.

In Germany, theatre productions by practitioners of colour have usually been categorised as so-called 'migrant theatre', an exclusionary term that implies that productions by directors and actors of migrant descent are not considered a part of 'German' theatre, but as something external and alien to German culture (Petersen and Schramm 2017, 4–5). As an act of defiance and a gesture of cultural critique, Langhoff and her circle began to label their work 'postmigrant theatre' to claim the recognition they deserved and to stress that their work is also part of German culture. In 2013, after some successful years at Ballhaus Naunynstraße, Langhoff moved to the leadership of the established, state-funded Maxim Gorki Theatre in Berlin. Since then, the Gorki Theatre has been voted 'Theatre of the Year' in Germany twice (2014, 2016), a gesture of public recognition that testifies to the innovative and empowering effect of postmigrant theatre (Schramm et al. 2019, 3–4).

As the artistic director of the Ballhaus theatre, Langhoff appears to have used the term as an act of defiant self-labelling, but also, as Stewart (2017, 57) has pointed out, as a means of establishing a strong profile for her theatre in the competitive Berlin theatre market. Langhoff used the word postmigrant as what she described as a 'term for doing battle with' (quoted in Stewart 2017, 57). This suggests that the term is more important for the work it can do than as a descriptor for a particular genre of theatre or category of people. The work that the term postmigrant theatre can do is twofold. Firstly, it has questioned existing knowledge frameworks: it has spurred critical reflection on prejudice and discrimination against migrants. Secondly, it has shifted these frameworks: it has inspired new perspectives and stories, particularly stories told by practitioners who are racialised or labelled 'migrants'. Langhoff herself has stressed this asset of the Ballhaus theatre's productions:

> For us postmigrant means that we critically question the production and reception of stories about migration and about migrants which have been available up to now and that we view and produce these stories anew, inviting a new reception.
>
> (quoted in Stewart 2017, 57)

Although the artist Jeannette Ehlers has not explicitly linked her work to the idea of postmigration, but rather, to the post-colonial and the decolonial, I contend that Langhoff's words also capture what is at stake in Ehlers' artistic practice, as one who seeks to critically examine the historical archive and create new ways of telling stories that invite a new reception.

The German discourse on postmigration

Before I turn to Ehlers' practice, I wish to proffer some further theoretical remarks. One of the assets of the concept of postmigration is the performative work that it can do, i.e. its ability to initiate a *process* of questioning and reinvention. This is evident from its academic trajectory: the idea gathered meaning and was elaborated theoretically around 2010, as it moved from a theatre practice informed by theory into the theoretical discussions of the social sciences and the humanities. The term postmigrant had been used for a long time in medicine and the social sciences as a relatively neutral descriptor for 'descendants of migrants'. Langhoff and her team at the Ballhaus theatre injected the term with a new political meaning. They deliberately used it to provoke the dominant public and media discourses on migration and to question the common perception of the migrant as 'the Other', that is to say, the migrant is perceived as a 'foreign body' that is not recognised as belonging to the imagined community of the nation. Today, the term postmigration is also associated with an analytical perspective on a social condition characterised by mobility and diversity. As an analytical perspective, postmigration engages with the struggles, societal transformations and processes of identifications taking place *after* migration – while recognising that migration is obviously still going on.

One of the most vociferously contested arenas in postmigrant societies concerns identity. Identity is also a classic subject in performance, theatre and the visual arts. A postmigrant perspective invites us to think about identity and belonging in dynamic and complex ways. It inspires us to move away from old notions of national and individual identity as uniform and static, as well as from simplistic ideas of belonging as being an attachment to one culture and one nation only. Instead, we must adopt an understanding of identity and belonging as open-ended processes of shifting identifications. We also need, the postmigrant perspective insists, to pay attention to the complex or intersectional nature of identification, i.e. to develop an awareness of how multiple forms of identification and discrimination are interlinked and bear down on individuals in different ways.

Migratory aesthetics

I would like to stress the relative newness of the postmigrant perspective within the arts: presently, there is no clearly defined toolbox for postmigrant cultural analysis, so we have to devise and test the concepts and approaches we use as we go along. In this regard, the postmigrant perspective differs from the, by now well-established, postcolonial perspective. Therefore, I would like to introduce a concept from art theory that I think can help us develop and clarify a postmigrant perspective in performance studies: migratory aesthetics.

Cultural theorist and video artist Mieke Bal introduced the concept of migratory aesthetics around 2005 (Bal 2007; Bal and Hernández-Navarro 2007; Bal 2015). Since then, the term has spread in scholarly discourses on the arts. Migratory aesthetics offers an alternative to categories such as migrant art and migrant theatre, which are problematic because they suggest that the producers of the works are migrants and thus belong to a category of citizens and cultural producers who are often not considered full members of society. Terms such as migrant art and migrant theatre tend to situate the creators of the works as outsiders. In other words, such terms have exclusionary effects. Conversely, the term migratory aesthetics refers to the aesthetic character of *the work itself* and the aesthetic *experience* of an audience. It thus provides a better frame for understanding the aesthetic and political dimensions of art and culture created by individuals with a migrant background, or indeed by individuals exploring the topic of migration without having a migrant background themselves.

The term thus helps us to focus our discussions on the interrelations between artworks and migration. Bal herself has described the concept of migratory aesthetics as a ground for analytical experimentation that can open up possible relations between the artwork and 'the migratory'. In Bal's understanding 'the migratory' is 'a quality of the world in which mobility is no longer the exception but on its way to becoming the standard' (Bal 2007, 23; see also Petersen 2017, 56–59). This means that it is on its way to becoming normal, something many people have experienced in one way or another. As the discourse on migratory aesthetics is not so much concerned with the artist, but rather with the work, the idea of migratory aesthetics as a feature of art resonates with the idea of the postmigratory as a feature of society rather than a label attributed to people of migrant descent.

The postcolonial and the decolonial

Although this is not the place to consider in depth postcolonial theory and its impact on the arts, I wish to make a brief remark on the relationship between postcolonial and decolonial approaches, as they are both important to Jeannette Ehlers' work. Postcolonial thinking is sometimes seen as a tradition of critique aimed at Western colonialism, and its accompanying institutions and ideas. It emerged out of the writings of thinkers concerned with imperialist race-relations and mindsets, such as Franz Fanon and Edward Said, and theorists associated with subaltern studies, most famously Gayatri Spivak. Postcolonial approaches have played an important part in devising a language to describe difference and hybridisation in and between cultures. Even so, these approaches have tended to remain fixated on notions of difference, dissidence, oppression and marginality, and this fixation has had the adverse effect of perpetuating a Western tradition of othering (Ong 1999, 34). Nevertheless, postcolonialism's strong political focus on difference and on the silencing of histories of oppression and racism makes its points of view very relevant to Ehlers' work, as I shall show.

Like postcolonial theory, decolonial theory emphasises the interconnection between modernity and coloniality. Coloniality constitutes what decolonial theorist Walter D. Mignolo has described as the 'the darker side of Western modernity' (2011, 2–3). In his view, coloniality and modernity are two sides of the same coin, but, according to Mignolo, Western thinkers have prioritised one side, modernity. Mignolo thus considers Western thinking misleading, and he states that racialised and previously colonised people need to emancipate themselves mentally. Compared to postcolonial theory, decolonial theory is thus more concerned with the decolonisation of the mind (Mignolo 2007, 450, 459).

Another important difference between postcolonial and decolonial approaches is that decolonial thinking puts a strong emphasis on art and aesthetics as a means of emancipation, and decolonial discourse in art and theory has significant purchase in dialogues between artists, curators and intellectuals from Latin America, the Caribbean and the diasporic communities in the US, Europe and beyond (Mignolo and Vázquez 2013). Contrary to many postcolonial scholars, Mignolo also insists on the need to 'delink' from Western ways of thinking. This method of delinking can perhaps be seen as an academic and artistic parallel to civil disobedience, where large groups of people refuse to obey certain laws or perform other forms of peaceful, but effective and transformative, protest.

The artistic practice of Jeannette Ehlers

Jeannette Ehlers is one of a number of contemporary artists who take a postcolonial or decolonial approach to formerly overlooked or suppressed histories, which have never been acknowledged as parts of 'national' history. The Kingdom of Denmark-Norway was engaged in the transatlantic slave trade and, in the context of this discussion, the trade in enslaved people – upon which the colonial plantation systems in the Caribbean and the continental Americas was built – must be considered one of the most gruesome forms of forced migration. Ehlers examines the archives of Danish colonialism with a view to increasing public recognition of the country's involvement, especially Denmark's part in the slave trade and chattel slavery in what was formerly known as the colony of the Danish West Indies, and is today known as the US Virgin Islands.

In recent years, Ehlers has created works in which she seeks to strike a balance between critical interrogation and affective evocation of the history of enslaved Africans.

Having a Danish mother and a father who was born in Trinidad, she is herself a descendant of enslaved Africans. It is Ehlers' identification with the Caribbean that has fostered her engagement in the history of slavery. Moreover, Ehlers' approach is informed by an anti-racist awareness of the Western history of racism that can be traced to colonialism and continues to the present. Despite her strong political and antiracist engagement, Ehlers' works are always open to different interpretations. There is also a distinct participatory – and thus performative - dimension to her works, as she often engages her audiences in different forms of active encounter.

Jeannette Ehlers' performance, *Whip It Good*

Ehlers first performed *Whip It Good* at the Ballhaus Naunynstraße theatre – the breeding ground of postmigrant theatre. She was commissioned to create *Whip It Good* by Art Labour Archives and Ballhaus Naunynstraße, as an artistic contribution to the event 'BE.BOP: Decolonizing the "Cold" War' in 2013. BE.BOP is an acronym for Black Europe Body Politics. It was a recurring decolonial curatorial initiative by the founder of the art agency Art Labour Archives, Alanna Lockward, who was a Berlin-based curator, writer and scholar. Walter Mignolo was an advisor and a regular participant since BE.BOP's inception in 2012, so here there is a direct connection between Ehlers and Mignolo as a protagonist of decolonial thinking.

Since 2013, the impact of *Whip It Good* has been heightened by Ehlers' re-enactment of the performance in, among other places, the US, the UK and Denmark. Moreover, her audiences have included people of colour as well as white people, such as myself. In what follows, I will focus on the first performance at the Ballhaus theatre. In her solo performance, Ehlers re-enacted one of the slavery era's most brutal forms of punishment – flogging – as a symbolic act. What was punished was not an enslaved person, but a white canvas. Associations with white skin and painting as a Western hegemonic art form came readily to mind. In the performance, Ehlers alternated between flogging the white canvas and rubbing the whip with black charcoal, so that as more black strokes were imprinted on the pristine canvas from the whip, the darker it became.

At the same time, Ehlers re-enacted a tradition that was, and still is, practiced across the continent of Africa: that of using the skin as a black canvas to be decorated with body paint on important social occasions. Inspired by West African rituals, Ehlers employed white paint to symbolise cleansing. The white also linked her body with the canvas while simultaneously stressing its differences. The body paint was white, but it was a paler shade of white than that of the canvas. As body painting, it was also infused with different connotations: ritual action, embodiment and temporariness, as opposed to the abstraction and permanence of the 'disembodied' canvas.

The postcolonial and the postmigrant perspectives intersect, but they also diverge in some respects. Therefore, I regard them as complementary, and I find it very useful to combine them. Ehlers' work is usually read as a de- and postcolonial practice. A de- and postcolonial perspective is arguably very apt for framing the social and historical critique articulated by Ehlers. However, seeing her work through the lens of postmigration means that her work can be appreciated at the same time for the way in which it

contributes to the development of new frames for understanding contemporary societies. In other words, a postmigrant perspective can help us to comprehend why a
performance like *Whip It Good* should not be seen merely
as a critique of a colonial past but also as a creative reimagination of history that inspires us to change things in the
present.

The performance also introduced another way of 'doing'
critical art. This was partly due to the way Ehlers engaged
her audience. The performance at the Ballhaus theatre
included the participation of a live audience. The performance developed into a collective ritual of transformation
or, better, a rite of passage that could ideally lead from a
state of oblivion to a new state of historical awareness and
spiritual liberation. After a thorough flogging of the canvas,
Ehlers ended her performance by inviting the audience to
help her to 'finish the work', handing the whip to those
who volunteered. This was the transgressive and transformative moment when the character of the work changed from
a performance art piece to a participatory event that engaged the audience as co-actors in a performative critique
of history. The piece thus enacted a 'working through' the
past and engendered solidarity and empathy between artist
and audience members.

Many spectators – of different colours and backgrounds –
have been deeply moved by *Whip It Good*. For some, it can
be argued that the work awakened a new consciousness.
The question is *how?* To answer this question, I would like
to invoke memory studies scholar Marianne Hirsch's notion of postmemory. As opposed to history, the notion of
memory denotes 'embodied experience in the process of
transmission' (Hirsch 2008, 111). Following Hirsch, I use

the term postmemory in the broad sense as referring to the 'guardianship' of a traumatic or genocidal past with which some people have what Hirsch describes as 'a living connection' (2008, 104). Can postmemories of slavery and colonialism be transformed into action and decolonial emancipation? I am sure that Ehlers' answer would be 'Yes!' Seen from a postmigrant perspective, the rite of passage that *Whip It Good* enacted draws the contours of a new pluralist and connective paradigm of cultural identity and memory, precisely because it draws on postmemory. According to Hirsch, postmemory's connection to the past is not mediated by recall, but it can be mediated by cultural representations, for example by representations of the slavery era in film where flogging scenes often figure prominently, for instance *12 Years A Slave* (2013), by British artist and filmmaker Steve McQueen. In other words, postmemory is fuelled by imaginative investment in and projection into the past. Thus, it is not identical to memory. It is disconnected from actual, personal memories, i.e. it is 'post'. At the same time, it can approximate memory in its affective force, meaning that it can have a similar emotional impact to one's own memories (Hirsch 2008, 107, 109).[1] By letting her performance end in a participatory ritual, Ehlers enhanced the emotional and decolonising impact of the performance.

The migratory aesthetics of Jeannette Ehlers' *Into the Dark*

By way of a conclusion, I would like to offer some final remarks on Ehlers' first theatre production, *Into the Dark*, in order to shed more light on migratory aesthetics and how these can be used to connect a local context to the global to show that such transnational entanglements are at the core of local postmigrant culture. *Into the Dark* premiered in 2017 at a small theatre in Copenhagen named FÅR302. Although it was performed on a theatre stage, it was not a conventional play based on a narrative, but rather a multimedia performance with black performers only – and shown to a primarily white Copenhagen audience. *Into the Dark* took as its starting point a scene from the nineteenth-century play *The Mulatto* (1840) by the Danish author Hans Christian Andersen. In this scene, one of the protagonists, Paléme, who is a maroon (a fugitive black slave), is trying to convince his acquaintance Horatio to participate in a revolt against the plantocracy of colonial Martinique. Notably, this scene had been displaced in time and space, from nineteenth-century Martinique to contemporary New Orleans. And from a live performance on a theatre stage to a video-recorded performance in a public urban space. This scene thus connected colonial past and postcolonial present. It also connected the site in Copenhagen to other sites of black diaspora culture, in the Caribbean and the US. Moving between and interconnecting times and places in such a complex way is typical of migratory aesthetics. As such, *Into the Dark* highlights important aspects of studying the migratory and the postmigratory.

Firstly, the piece underscores the need for interdisciplinary approaches and the futility of isolating one artform from others: *Into the Dark* consisted of more than a poetic, fragmented series of performances and soundscapes, as it also included dance, poetry and video works. Secondly, its numerous references to black cultures highlighted an important point: art emerging from postmigrant conditions is at one and the same time engaged in local or national struggles – in this case a critique of Danish colonialism and racism – *and* transculturally connected to a wider world. In *Into the Dark*, this was evident from the many references to African diaspora aesthetics and histories that mixed with references to Danish colonialism and Danish racism. Thirdly, *Into the Dark* demonstrated that, more than anything else, Ehlers is engaging post- and decolonial critique. Yet, at the same time, the migratory aesthetics of her production emphasised transcultural connectivity, thus prying open the very notion of culture as a contained entity.

If we compare *Into the Dark* with postmigrant theatre, for example the Ballhaus theatre's production *Crazy Blood*, two things become clear: firstly, that a postmigrant lens can be applied to other forms of artistic expression than those explicitly labelled 'postmigrant'; and, secondly, that these forms may differ considerably. By moving from *Into the Dark* back to *Crazy Blood* we have come full circle, back to where I began, with postmigrant theatre and the question of what contemporary theatre, performance and art can bring to the debate on migration, culture and society. They have the potential not only to create critical counter-images, but also to envision ways out, not in the sense that the arts can solve social problems and political crises, but in the sense that they can be a means of exploring new ways of seeing and acting in the social and political world.

Acknowledgements

I would like to thank Emma Cox, editor of the volume *Performance and Migration* in the 4x45 series of Routledge's Digital Theatre+ video and publishing initiative; Andy Lavender, editor of the 4x45 Series; and the anonymous peer reviewer for constructive feedback on the first draft of the lecture.

Their expertise as performance and theatre scholars and their helpful suggestions for improvement have provided invaluable support. I would also like to extend my gratitude to my colleague cultural studies scholar and filmmaker Hans Christian Post for recording the lecture, and to Production Manager of Digital Theatre Stephen Quinn for his skilful editing of the footage.

Note

1 A note on the dichotomy between history and memory. Marianne Hirsch ties (post)memory to the aesthetic and institutional transmission of the spectrum of 'embodied knowledge absent from the historical archive (or perhaps merely neglected by traditional historians). For better or worse, these supplemental genres and institutions have been grouped under the umbrella term "memory"' (Hirsch 2008, 105). Hirsch's distinction between memory and history implies that, although Ehlers draws on the writings of history, her own artistic practice should rather be characterised as memory work, or better, postmemory work than historical knowledge production, as she seeks to adopt, reactivate and reembody distant social, archival and cultural memories by 'reinvesting them with resonant individual ... forms of mediation and aesthetic expression' (Hirsch 2008, 111).

2

Being second generation

Australian-Indian performers Raina Peterson and Sonya Suares in dialogue

Introduced, transcribed and edited by Paul Rae

Link | https://www.digitaltheatreplus.com/education/
collections/digital-theatre/being-second-generation-
indian-australian-performers-sonya

Introduction

Internationally, the headline news about migration in Australia most often concerns asylum seekers and refugees. In the early 2000s, Australia began to experience the knock-on effects of upheavals in the Middle East, with refugees making their way to Indonesia, and then attempting to reach the Australian island continent by boat. Governments of both main parties – Labor and the Liberal–National Coalition – responded by taking a hard line on undocumented seaborne arrivals, minimising and attempting to eliminate the chance that anyone arriving that way would be permitted to settle in Australia. Many boats were intercepted and turned back (Spinks 2018). Other migrants were taken for so-called 'offshore processing' on

DOI: 10.4324/9781003199755-2

the outlying Australian island of Christmas Island, on Manus Island in Papua New Guinea, and on the small and relatively remote Pacific island nation of Nauru. Successive Australian governments have insisted that these practices are to save lives: for as long as the boats were coming, people were drowning. However, the fate of those stuck in the limbo of indefinite detention – unable to return home, not permitted to move to Australia and unwilling to be resettled elsewhere – became a high-profile problem. Even a former Commissioner of the Australian Border Force noted in 2018 that there was a universal desire within government to resolve the problem, saying that although the policy had been highly effective in stopping the boats, offshore processing had descended into what he described as an 'almost insoluble mess' that was now a 'weeping sore on Australia's collective psyche' (Quaedvlieg 2018).

The situation is hugely challenging in terms of policy, practicality and morality, and theatre-makers have consistently played a role in bringing the plight of refugees and asylum seekers to light for Australian audiences. In a 2008 article, Tom Burvill characterised multiple productions on asylum as 'interventions impelled by ethical outrage at what was being done "in our name" by the [then] Howard Government' (234). That trend has continued, as work by Emma Cox, Caroline Wake and others has showed (see Cox 2015; Cox and Wake 2018; Wake 2019). And yet, while the asylum issue rightly demands our attention, it risks eclipsing the larger story of migration to Australia. Hidden behind headlines about tough border policing is the fact that Australia remains a major migrant destination. New arrivals entering either through the humanitarian or migration programs make up about 64% of Australia's population growth (Simon-Davies 2018). I am one of them: I arrived in Australia in 2014 – one of the 178,000 new arrivals for that year (Phillips and Simon-Davies 2017).

The story of migration to Australia is itself a complex and in many ways troubling one. The roots of Australia as it we know it today lie in the establishment of a penal colony by the British in 1788. As transportation of convicts from Britain to Australia continued, and settlers began to arrive from Britain and other parts of Europe, Australia's indigenous populations were violently dispossessed of their land: many died from imported diseases; others were put to work or corralled into reservations; and children were removed from their families and communities and put up for adoption by white families. Still others were hunted down and killed. Australia continues to live with the legacy of this.

Meanwhile, over the course of the nineteenth century, economic migrants began to arrive in significant numbers from other places. Pacific Islanders, mainly from Vanuatu and the Solomon Islands, worked in sugar-cane plantations; North Indians and those from neighbouring regions such as Afghans rode camel trains across the vast Australian outback; and a gold rush in the second half of the nineteenth century brought many Chinese to seek their fortunes in the goldfields of Western and Southeastern Australia.

Theatre came too. In a sense, all non-Indigenous performance in the nineteenth century was migrant performance, though perhaps one of the most interesting cases is Chinese opera: for instance, as Harold Love reports, fourteen Cantonese opera companies applied for theatrical licences between 1858 and 1870, to entertain the mainly Cantonese-speaking miners, and provide some respite from work that was difficult, often unprofitable and sometimes dangerous (Love 1985, 71). The Chinese in particular were periodically subject to attack by miners of British and Irish origin.

These attitudes set the tone of things to come. Australia was federated into a single nation state in 1901, and introduced the Immigration Restriction Act, better known as the 'White Australia Policy', which would not be conclusively abolished until 1973. The policy sought to limit migration to Australia to those of European origin, and numbers of migrants from other places dropped precipitously. The picture changed from the 1970s, when multiculturalism began to be embraced, and specific events like the Vietnam War, which Australia fought in, led to the arrival of large numbers of so-called 'boat people' from Vietnam. From the late 1990s, the legacy of the White Australia Policy has reared its head in the form of white nationalism within both fringe and mainstream political parties, but migration continues – and continues to diversify. While the largest number of migrants to Australia continues to come, like me, from the UK, the overall composition of the migrant population is changing significantly. In 1954, migrants from the UK made up almost 50% of the total; today, that figure is about 18%, followed by New Zealand, China, India and the Philippines (Simon-Davies 2018, Table 2: Top 10 countries of birth).

It is now almost half a century since the end of the White Australia Policy – time for multiple generations of Australians of migrant origin to be born, grow up, and, amongst many other things, to become theatre-makers and performers. In this film, we hear from two Australia-born artists of Indian origin who have responded to, and continue to act upon, their ethnic heritage in overlapping but distinct ways. The story of Indian migration to Australia is a long one, whose complexity mirrors that of the larger migration story. Indians came to Australia in the nineteenth century as camel drivers and through the networks of the British Empire, working as agricultural labourers, domestic workers, and itinerant hawkers. Some resident Indians remained during the era of the White Australia Policy, but the 1954 census recorded only about 2,500 Indians in the country (Bilimoria 2015, 11). That changed with the end of the policy: professionals including doctors, teachers, computer programmers and engineers began migrating from India in increasing numbers, while others of ethnic Indian origin came from other parts of the former British Empire, such as Malaysia, and particularly from Fiji, descendants of an indentured labour scheme that ran there from the late nineteenth to the early twentieth century. By the early 1980s, the number of Indians in Australia had increased to about 41,000. Labour shortages in the early 2000s saw a new influx of migrants from India, more than doubling the India-born population by 2016. In that year, 675,658 people claimed Indian ancestry, constituting 2.8% of the Australian population (Department of Foreign Affairs and Trade 2018, 360).

The two artists featured here are both Australia-born second-generation migrants whose parents arrived during that first post-White Australia Policy period. Sonya Suares is an actor working in television and mainstream and independent theatre. Raina Peterson teaches and practices the South Indian classical dance form of Mohiniyattam, and also makes experimental dance and queer cabaret with their company, Karma Dance. The dialogue that follows reflects on Suares and Peterson's experiences growing up as the children of migrants, coming to grips with familial inheritance and local racism. It traces the development of artist-activist identities and queer aesthetics, and offers insights into how industry practices and politics shape the life of an artist. The transcript has been edited for clarity.

An interview with SONYA SUARES and RAINA PETERSON

Growing up in Australia

SONYA SUARES: My parents came out in the 1970s to Australia from Mumbai in India. My mother's brother was working as a country doctor in Shepparton,[1] and my mum came out there because in the late 1960s and 70s, as now, there were not enough doctors and teachers in the country. My grandfather had worked his way up in that traditional rags to riches story as a respected surgeon in Mumbai, and you can probably read between the lines that his eldest son could have been a doctor in India, but he moved to the furthest place on earth, so there's a little bit of family trauma there. Then somebody suggested to my mum while my dad was studying in the United States, 'why not come and teach, you know, your brother's in Australia'. So she moved to this place she'd really never heard of, and taught in Echuca and Shepperton and I think also in Mooroopna. Then she came back to India, married my dad, and they came out together *just* after the White Australia Policy, and they had really different experiences of the landscape here. My mother is an extrovert: charming, and can talk to anybody. But my dad was an introvert and the gender roles didn't really suit them at all. She was trapped in suburbia with the kids, and he had to go and work in the workplace and he had this really difficult relationship with Australia. He's never given up his Indian citizenship. He came in 1975. He's spent most of his life here, but he will still say, 'I was in a supermarket and there were these Australians in front of me'. And I'll be like, 'yeah, really? In Australia, there are Australians in front of you in the supermarket? What a frigging shock, dad!' But it still remains this foreign place.

Then they moved to the city [Melbourne] for Dad's work, and I grew up in Glenwaverly, in the Southeastern suburbs, which were super-white when I was growing up there. Esther Wong and I were the only non-white kids at Mimosa Primary School as I remember it. And someone had gone to the trouble — I used to walk home — of graffitiing the slipways that have 'no entry' signs with 'Smart little Indians, No entry', just so I could clock that all the way home. And I remember as a kid thinking 'that's unfortunate!' But it was pretty pointed.

RAINA PETERSON: My mum's Fiji Indian and her family have been in Fiji for several generations. Originally from India, but we don't actually know where in India we're from. And I'm not quite sure why we don't, because there are plenty of Fiji Indians who are like, 'yeah, we're Gujarati' and they've retained this…

SS: … cultural identity.

RP: Yes. But we don't have any sense of what our regional identity in India actually was and I don't know whether that's because of trauma or what, but as far as I can see there's a complete lack of curiosity about where in India we're originally from. My ancestors were indentured labourers working on sugar cane plantations in Fiji. And every now and then I try researching the indentured labourer experience and it's actually quite devastating and I end up not doing that, because it's just quite upsetting to know that your ancestors were exposed to all this violence. We don't really talk about it in my family and my community that much.

SS: It's funny that way with trauma isn't it? I sort of glossed over that thing of my uncle coming to Shepparton – it's not in the narrative. It's:'and then he came to Shepparton!'

RP: No 'why'.

SS: No 'why'. No unpacking that stuff. I think that there's a coping mechanism in that.

RP: So I guess my relationship with India as a country is still abstract for me. I've only been there once. And that was partly as a tourist and partly to receive training in dance. But it's never been as 'India, the Motherland'. I guess I and my family, my community, feel very strongly connected with Fiji.

SS: I'm really curious about the idea that your parents created a dance community around you in Gippsland.[2] That's amazing!

RP: I need to go back a bit, to get there. My parents met in Niue, which is a tiny island in the South Pacific. It's a quarter of the size of Tasmania.[3] Most people in Australia have never heard of it unless they are Pasifika. My mum studied teaching at university and after she graduated she went to teach at the high school in Niue. And my dad was also a teacher from country Victoria and he …

SS: … it's a theme.

RP: It's a theme: everyone's a teacher in country Victoria! So he did Volunteers Overseas, where people from developed countries go to Third World countries and do their profession there. My mum and dad were teaching at the same high school in Niue, and that's how they met.

SS: Cute.

RP: Then they got married in Fiji, and moved back to country Victoria.

SS: When you were growing up, did you ever have regrets about what would have happened if they'd stayed in Fiji – what your life would have been like, imaginatively?

RP: Yes. I think it would have also been a bit weird, being mixed race. But probably less violent than my childhood.

SS: Yeah.

RP: Part of the reason we moved to country Victoria is because, it's what my dad knew – it's where his family's from – but also because they wanted teachers there. My mum migrated in the early 1980s, and shortly afterwards more Fiji Indians came to regional Victoria, mostly as teachers. We connected eventually and formed a little community organisation, meeting together regularly and doing religious and cultural things. So I grew up with quite a strong community around me. I think it's only now I'm starting to appreciate how unusual that was.

SS: I used to be a bit jealous of other migrant children who seemed to be super-connected to their religious tradition or a sense of culture, because we were in a real no man's land. My parents are Catholic, so even going back, three, four generations, English was the first language for my family. I remember asking my grandfather, 'what kind of music do you like?' And he reeled off Mozart, Brahms … they were very western in their outlook, even in India. So coming here, they were visibly Other, but didn't have a connection with people who'd migrated from Mumbai or the surrounding area: there was no practice of culture, there was nothing to hang that on. We just had aunties and uncles, which was great – but nothing like a dance community. We spoke English. Did you speak any Gujarati?

RP: We spoke Fiji Hindi. And I say 'we', but I didn't. When my mum came here, I can't imagine how isolated and lonely she must have felt, and people were really racist then. People didn't know what 'Indian' was. When I was at school people thought I was Native American because that's what they thought 'Indian' meant. They only knew what 'Indian' meant when *The Simpsons* came about and then Apu's character …

SS: Oh God, that awesome cultural ambassador of Apu[4] …

RP: … so then they knew: 'oh, this is what Indian is, this is how we should be racist to an Indian – right, got it. Now I know who you are.'

SS: Culturally specific racism. Awesome.

RP: Yeah, I experienced an enormous amount of racism from a very young age, which was quite awful. So on the one hand I had this really strong Fijian and community connection, but I was also dealing with intense racism and it was hard to process who I was. And because my mum spoke Fiji Hindi and my dad doesn't, I grew up speaking English, but it was peppered with Hindi. When I was about seven, I was being bullied for being brown, but also for speaking Hindi at school without meaning to, and without realising that no one else understood me. I think that at seven is when I realised: 'OK, being Indian is bad.' And I had all this internalised racism around what it means to be Indian, and I just stopped speaking Hindi.

SS: I had a similar experience actually, round about that same age. There was a girl at my primary school, and she would come up to me every now and then and say, 'Sonya, have you decided whether you're Indian or Australian?' This was a big thing for her. And it was a big existential thing for me, too. My parents kept taking us back to India because they had this massive cultural nostalgia for it. They didn't have a lot of money. They didn't buy us a lot of things, but they would save up and take us back to India. And it was such an extraordinary thing to be in a land where suddenly everyone looks like you, and you're not conspicuous. I just saw your body when you talked about your mother and how extraordinary it must have been for her, and your whole body tensed up. That's what it feels like when you just ... you have your dukes up a little bit, you know, to combat that sort of stuff. And then the feeling of just being able to just *be*, and look like everybody else is extraordinary for a child.

Becoming a performer

SS: So you danced in Gippsland with this community of Fijian Indians. Was that the foundation of your practice?

RP: Absolutely. Our community would connect for cultural and religious events and one year for Diwali[5] someone was like, 'let's teach the kids a dance'. So one of the aunties taught us a dance and we performed it in this little community hall in Morwell.[6] That was my first dance performance. I was five and I was all dressed up in these costumes that my mum sewed out of things that she bought from Spotlight.[7]

SS: God bless her.

RP: It was a really beautiful moment for me, and I think that was the beginning. Every year we would do all these dance classes and learn performances for the Diwali concert.

SS: How did your mum find a teacher? My mum roped me in to maybe three months of Bharatanatyam[8] when I was

eight years old, and she found a friend who practiced it,
but what kind of …

RP: It was just a mishmash of different things. It was folk
dance and Bollywood, and they tried to incorporate elements of Bharatanatyam that they learnt from films. It
was Indian, but it was drawing from all these different
things. And because my mum was on a crusade about
how racist and monocultural everyone was, she would
make me and my sibling perform, for the school. She
would organise that, and we got a bit bullied for it.

So that was how I started formally. I just really loved
to dance. And then when I was eleven, we ran out
of aunties who were willing to take over the task of
teaching us dance routines, so my parents were on the
lookout for an Indian dance school. Being in Gippsland,
there was nothing. But they happened to come across
an article in the newspaper about Tara Rajkumar's latest
production. It was called *Mahamaya* and it was at the Alexander Theatre.[9] It was an interview with her and my
parents were like, 'oh yeah, let's go and check this out'.
We went to see it and it was *amazing*: it was so incredible. It was this contemporary Indian dance production
and I just remember very vividly this image of Tara Rajkumar: she's got this long wavy black hair and, in this
dance, she disembowels a demon and drinks his blood
and I was like, 'woah, that's amazing. I want to be her'.

SS: 'I want that.'

RP: 'I want that.' So my parents signed us up in her dance
school and at the time Taranji was the only Mohiniyattam teacher in all Australia. So it's completely random
that I got trained in this obscure form of classical Indian
dance which originates from Kerala.

SS: And you've been disembowelling demons ever since! And that happenstance of how your practice grows out of opportunity ... that was the opportunity available.

RP: We still lived in Warragul,[10] so twice a week my dad would drive me and [my sibling] Kav to the city – and it would take at least an hour and a half one way – and then drive us back. I did my arangetram in Mohiniyattam in 2010, which is like the debut, solo graduation concert.

Another moment in my life which was quite important for me and helped me decide that I wanted to be a dancer was an initiative organised by Ausdance[11] where they connected professional dancers with cultural dance schools to develop a dance that combined the professional dancer's practice with the ethnic dancers'. My dance school, Tara Rajkumar's dance school Natya Sudha, was connected with Jacob Boehme, who's an amazing Indigenous contemporary dancer. So me and three other people from Taranji's school, and Taranji herself, worked with Jacob to create this really amazing dance. And in that process, what we danced was great, but I think what was exciting for me was meeting Jacob and thinking here's a person of colour who's a professional dancer, and I think that planted the seed in me to be like, 'oh yeah, I can be that too'.

SS: 'I could be that too, *here*.' Like, he is in the landscape, here. It's that thing, isn't it? That classic representation line: if you can see it, you can be it.

RP: Absolutely.

SS: Even if he's not Indian or Fijian Indian, he's a person of colour with a practice that has an audience here. That's so powerful, that idea. And when you're that impressionable, and you're trying to work out if it is even is a thing you

can do. How did your parents take it when you said you
wanted to [be a dancer]? Because they set you up, right?

RP: They set me up; they had this coming! When I was at
University, me and two of my friends got together because we were really frustrated by the racism we were
experiencing in the world around us and we said, 'let's
do something about this! What should we do? A forum?
A magazine? Do we publish something? What's our action? What's our product?' And one of us said, 'let's do
a cabaret show', and I thought 'great'. So we did this
anti-racist cabaret show called Ladies of Colour Agency,
and it had legs. We had two full length shows, took it to
Adelaide – Adelaide hated us; that's fine, we hated them
too. I did this act where I'm wearing the Australian flag
and I cut it off my body in a kind of burlesque … And
they were enraged.

SS: Don't cut the flag.

RP: We were on the Channel 9 news…

SS: And not in a good way.

RP: Not in a good way. And it was all very exciting. So I think
that was another key milestone in me becoming a performer, because I was performing professionally. But yes,
I think my parents were like, 'ah yeah, Raina likes dancing, that's nice. Nice hobby'. And then I was in the middle of doing my Honours thesis in anthropology, when
I was like, 'bugger this, I'm going to be a dancer'. And my
parents did not take that very well at all. They were not
very supportive of that. But in 2015 I did my first full-
length work with my dance partner Govind Pillai. It was
called *In Plain Sanskrit* – an experimental classical Indian
dance show. And my parents were just like: [*mimes proud,
appreciative clapping*] 'Yes. Yes! That's my child.'

SS: So when *they* could see it, *you* could be it!

RP: Totally!

SS: My parents were actually quite cool about it, to be honest, partly because they had no context. There were so many doctors in my family. And I was a smart kid and where I went to high school originally, that was the identity afforded me: the smart girl that sat up at the front of the class and got bullied a bit. And then I heard about this academic high school and realised that was my lifeboat out of the whole situation in Glen Waverly High. So I sat the exam and I got in. And there was no tap dancing or arias on that exam. But weirdly enough when I was in that environment with all of these bright women – it was a girl's school, The Mac.Robertson Girls' High[12] – you're afforded the opportunity of being more than one thing. So I looked up and I looked around and there was a bunch of really amazing budding artists at the school, and there were chorals, and musicals, and I said, 'well, I'll be doing that – that sounds amazing!'

I don't know if [my parents] didn't hear me right when I stopped saying I was going to be a doctor and started saying 'I'm going to be an actor' … Maybe they didn't hear the 'D' disappear out of that. But they never challenged me on it. They always said, 'you've just got to figure it out yourself'. And I think that's quite em-powering for a young person, you know, when you've got all the bluster of a teenager, and you [think you] know everything. You're like, 'yeah, I will'.

It was the 1990s as well, so multicultural Australia was an idea that we could all wrap our brains around. And I genuinely thought that I was going to be leading the charge and just have a career on telly. My first telly audition I got a role in – it remains to this day my only recurring role on telly – and it was a bit rock and roll because this show was shot up in Queensland in Port Douglas and in Port Melbourne.[13] And they were flying me up in Year 11 and I was like, 'this is the life for me – I'm going to live like this now!' And I probably didn't experience much of the hardship of it right up front, as a kid.

Then I just followed that trajectory. I heard about drama schools. I thought, 'I'll go to a drama school'. And I sang, so I thought, 'oh, I'll do music theatre'. And that was an odd decision. My parents were not super-creative. But they're storytellers and they love story. They love film, and the midday musical. So I did grow up with a diet of music theatre. So I just thought, 'I'll learn through different things and combine that into a practice'. It was *very* music theatre [at drama school]. But I think that was my experience: again, one non-white kid in this very didactic educational framework where I didn't really fit a box and they didn't really know what to do with me. My voice was a light soprano. I was not the sassy best friend. So coming out of drama school I really had to ask: 'where do I fit in in this place? Is it screen and telly?' Because by then the screens had whitened again, in the early part of the millennium. There was kind of a regression.

I had to start thinking, why do I want to do this if it's a space that I'm not allowed into very often, or only asked to play these bit-roles and stereotypes that are uncomfortable – Muslim doctor is one that I got a lot – because they have actually nothing to do with me. I mean, I'm not Muslim! It has to do with what's projected onto me: when people see me, they imagine this particular cultural heritage that I don't have. My sensibility's actually a lot broader than that stereotype. So if those are the stereotypes that I'm allowed to play, what am I doing here in this industry? What do I want to say? Who is my audience?

The seeds of coming out of drama school, the seeds of what is my practice now, were those provocations [and] I guess what led me to be an artist-activist. I saw you when you answered the question about becoming a dancer and you did this [*shows herself becoming more assertive*] in your body. I think that actually happens to you as you progress: you find yourself having a need to bust out of a stereotype that has been imposed and reclaim your voice. We all do this because it's our way of speaking to the world, right? I tell stories. I'm interested in unpacking identity. I'm interested in unpacking what it is to be human, *fully* human. So those roles that are complex and have arcs and trajectories – I want to play *those* people. I want to write about them, I want to tell stories that change people and shift things. Whether it be talking about climate change or social inclusion or unpacking philosophical questions. I think a lot of the questions we ask in theatre are deeply and profoundly philosophical.

So that's where I've found myself. This is my 25th year in this industry, and the work that I make and the work that I do around activism – I put a big circle around that – that's all my practice, because I think these are the ways that we tell stories within our sector.

Performing now

RP: I'm a dancer-choreographer. I draw on the techniques and aesthetics of classical Indian dance to create my work. I've now got four full-length works, which are all quite different from each other. *In Plain Sanskrit* (2015) was my first full length work and that's an experimental classical Indian dance. *Bent Bollywood* (2018) is a queer cabaret show that's looking at gender and sexuality. *Third Nature* (2019) is a contemporary dance work. And *Kāla* (2019) is a classical Indian dance show about death. I draw on Bollywood [and] Hindu iconography, mythology and practice a lot. I've performed around the queer scene for about ten years and queer performance art is a really strong influence: it's also where I situate a certain part of my body of work.

My last full-length work was *Third Nature*, which is an exploration of gender and sexuality, and diaspora and identity. It uses the motif of jasmine to represent gender, because in my culture jasmine has strong associations with femininity and sexuality. It's used to adorn marriage beds and to decorate weddings, and women wear jasmine in their hair. Jasmine's an aphrodisiac, and it's got these really sensual properties. We had this set that was an enormous structure made from paper strands of jasmine and, during the course of the work, we would interact with this set and play with it with lighting as it interacted with the music, and dance in it out of it. There's projection and shadows, and it was really quite beautiful. I guess we were trying to envision a future world or an alternate timeline where gender doesn't exist, there are no binaries and there was no colonisation: trying to create a beautiful world where there aren't those limitations around violence and binaries.

SS: And thought.

RP: And thought.

SS: These are the kinds of things that I'm interested in as well. It just takes different forms. I run a small theatre independent music theatre company [called 'Watch This'], which is dedicated to the work of Stephen Sondheim. On the face of it, it seems super-mainstream – he has a very traditional form in some ways. But what draws me to Sondheim's work is that he is a humanist, and his work is incredibly diverse. You get *Pacific Overtures* (1976), which is an American composer-lyricist creating a work set in Japan at the moment of western incursion hundreds of years ago, from the perspective of the Japanese. It's an incredible kind of imaginative exercise and in some ways it reframes the notion of fear of invasion. You know, we performed that work in an election year and the rhetoric of 'stop the boats' was really quite intense – still continues to be.[14] In this play, a lowly samurai and fisherman are sent to literally stop the boats of western incursion in this work, which looks at the human need to hang on to constraints and the ideas around culture and boundary, and then what happens next when you don't – the last song in the work is 'Next'.

When I'm not producing Sondheim musicals, I spend a lot of time in the development of new Australian writing, and two of the most cherished works that I've done in recent times help answer the questions: Who do I do work for? Who do I produce work for? Who do I want to speak to? One of [the works] was *Melbourne*

Talam (2017) which was produced by Melbourne Theatre Company.[15] It traces the stories of three Indian immigrants, and told their stories in a non-linear fashion. It was for the Education season – so these incredibly diverse cohorts of young people in Melbourne came to that work. And then it went out on the road to places like Mildura and Wodonga.[16] It was in Wodonga there was like one Indian kid in the audience. And you saw her response to this work: it was like you in Gippsland, right? She asked a question and she could barely articulate it at Q+A time, because it was clearly so meaningful to her. You know, that hits you.

Or earlier this year, when beautiful Fleur Kilpatrick wrote a play that won the Max Afford Playwrights' Award in 2018 called *Whale*. She wrote this role for me as this protagonist, almost antagonist, character, Sonya, and the titular role in this in this work, 'Whale', was played by Chanella Macri. Sarah Walker was the third person in the triangle. But really the two load-bearing roles were myself and Chanella – both women of colour carrying this story forward, which is a call to action about the climate emergency. And you again see young people having a visceral experience and being changed by theatre. That's the kind of work that I feel is meaningful and that I want to make.

Being an artist

RP: Earlier, Sonya, you were talking about how there was a time when you were feeling hopeful about multicultural representation, and you were going to ride that wave, and then everything became whitewashed. I think something similar happened in dance as well, because in the late 1980s and 90s classical Indian dance and contemporary Indian dance was everywhere. It was a really great time: Dr Chandrabhanu and Tara Rajkumar and another person – I think her name's Padma Menon – were doing these amazing productions in mainstream venues including the Victorian Arts Centre.[17] They were touring professional companies all over the place and it was really quite extraordinary. And then there was the Howard government, and all these cuts to …

SS: I was about to say, 'I'll tell you what happened – John Howard happened'.[18]

RP: Yeah. He happened, and it affected the whole arts industry, but it particularly affected culturally diverse artists. Now there's very little, [but] when I did *In Plain Sanskrit* in 2015, there was no Indian dance in mainstream venues. It was actually quite scary for me and Govind to produce this work. Because we were like, 'OK, what even is this? Who's going to come and see this?' We didn't think anyone would come, but we sold out. It was amazing, and after we did, there was a lot of conversation by people in a similar situation to us – second generation, emerging artists, trained in non-western art forms, classical Indian dance – just getting very excited about it. So, it's really interesting: I'm an emerging artist. I've been an emerging artist for ten years and, with the current situation in the arts industry, I'll probably remain an emerging artist for my entire career!

SS: As long as you don't end up being a subsiding artist! You know, I always think that counterpoint [is]: what do you emerge to and how does that get sustained? The whole mid-career artist issue. I'm technically mid-career. I mean, I don't know what happens, after you emerge.

RP: Exactly. I think something absolutely needs to change with the arts industry, because I love what I'm doing, but it's really not sustainable. I need to be able to get paid for my work and I need to have the time and the resources to do what I do. One of my heroes is Akram Khan, who is a London-based Kathak dancer. He's got this amazing company and he churns out all these incredible productions and tours all over the place and … oh my God, I love him so much and … and *I could be Akram Khan!*

SS: You could!

RP: And not just me. There are hundreds of classical Indian dancers in Melbourne. There are dozens of classical Indian dance schools just in Melbourne. And if there was the support by the industry, there could be so many Akram Khans here, you know?

SS: There really could. Then there's companies like Indian Ink [in New Zealand] or Tamasha theatre company in London, where there are Indian creatives leading work that's about the subcontinental community, because theatre in London is thriving [and] it can sustain and support these kinds of delineations within that industry, whereas I reckon what we have here is a scarcity mentality. I do a lot of my work in independent theatre practice and I'm most interested in that work in some ways. But I also want to eat! We are all basically clamouring for the same piddling amounts of grants to sustain an idea of a creative practice and not just a series of gigs. And that is a really important psychological distinction to make – that I have agency – to not just see my work as 'the skill-tester claw comes, and maybe it plonks me in a TV series and maybe it doesn't'. But you've also got to acknowledge that you're charting in this basically skeletal artistic framework that is suffering death by a thousand cuts.

The Howard years are very important because that's how the political drift of the national conversation started. People would never have thought it possible to get away with that alt-right rhetoric in Parliament that has proliferated in our cultural discourse. That has a real-world impact on practitioners and our art forms. Indian classical dance gets relegated to a community practice, and maybe bubbles up to one piece of main-stage programming once in a way, but who can live like that? I think if you are trying to mark in dot point the obstacles that we're working with, in the framework within which we're working, those barriers are very real.

RP: Yes. I think in the dance sector, 'dance' means 'western contemporary dance' with a silent 'western', and everything else is multicultural dance or community dance. I'm like, 'OK, so dance is western contemporary dance and ballet, and multicultural dance or whatever you want to call it is the rest of the world?' It's really centring and normalising a white, western way of producing work, and it's limiting. As an audience member, I don't want to keep seeing one kind of dance over and over and over again. It's not sustainable. The arts industry of *all* industries cannot be a monoculture! It cannot. It'll destroy itself. Arts needs to have vibrancy and diversity. It needs to have lots of ideas and people and ways of navigating the world, in itself, otherwise it cannot continue.

SS: And the way out of this circular logic is to look at who the stakeholders are. A lot of these mainstream companies and performing arts centres think upwards: that artistic directors report to boards, who are the stakeholders. These are the structures of white supremacy in our industry. A study has just come out that shows exactly how disproportionately white all our cultural institutions are, disproportionate to the population.[19]

But if you flipped the paradigm and you look at the stakeholders of art as being the audience, how do you nourish this practice? How do you make it bigger? How do you grow it for everyone? Invite those people into the theatre! And you invite them into the theatre by showing them that these stories are about you too. So, for example, I made the argument to Melbourne Theatre Company that if you put a stock image on the poster for *Melbourne Talam*, everybody's graphically literate – they know that it's a stock image. That's not even a Melbourne train, it's a Sydney train, and some brown chick holding a phone, right? But if you put *us*, the actual actors, and it's got the same branding as all the rest of the Melbourne Theatre Company shows, you're talking to your audience and you're telling them, 'this is not the education show, this is part of our season and our focus, and you're inviting those people into the theatre'. And the marketing team, god bless them, they were right on it and they used that thinking, and they have ever since. *Hungry Ghosts* the next year had Jing-Xuan Chan and Emina Ashman on the poster. Jing-Xuan was on the front of Melbourne Theatre Company's brochure this year with the new work *Golden Shield* (2019), which was my favourite work in the whole season.[20]

But to go the possibilities: having that conversation with your audience, inviting these people in as stakeholders in your practice, you have to go back to that idea of representation. And because of the conversations I was having anyway with my colleagues in mainstage institutions, I ended up being sucked onto the Equity Diversity Committee of our union, the MEAA (the Media Entertainment Arts Alliance). I ended up continuing the conversations I had had there, and we kept talking about representation and different activations: 'can we do something visual? Can we do something grassroots?', and so on.

2018 had been a shocking year for women in theatre in Australia because of the way in which the #MeToo movement here had hit some very present roadblocks in terms of speaking truth to power. Defamation laws don't work the same way in Australia as they do in the States. The onus is on the person making claims, so it actually puts this downward pressure on women in theatre who are trying to speak up about systemic inequality, and abuse and harassment. *Melbourne Talam* was in 2017, and at the end of the year, I thought, 'we should get all the *desi* people together, all the South Asian people, and have a pot-luck lunch at my place – I just want to meet these people'. I think probably because I wanted the childhood that you had, with the parents that would pull everyone together for Puja[21] or whatever, I was redoing that in my adulthood. So we had that all in, in 2017, and in 2018, I was like, 'bugger it, I'm just having the women!'

So in the middle of silly season, these fifteen women came and they decked out in Bollywood and we did a DIY *Vanity Fair* photo. And as I was doing it, I got in touch with about fifteen more women who couldn't make it, and I realised there are all these people practicing, and there was the kernel of this idea of this grassroots representation of 'just not that many'.

Because this is the excuse that's given all the time: 'oh, we absolutely meant to cast this person' or 'we absolutely wanted to foster this Indian classical dance practice that you're talking about, but there's just not that many, you know?' It comes up *all the time* and it occurred to me that this could be a visual rebuttal to that idea. It can happen from within communities, and the penicillin of that, the by-product, is that, while the title is a provocation to the wider industry, the act itself of engaging with your community, summoning your community together and taking this photo, is really joyous, it's energising.

RP: If I wanted to be really specific about who my target audience is, I would say it is second generation South Asians, particularly classical South Asian artists, but also queer people of colour. That's really who I'm creating my work for. I think that the work that I'm most excited about in terms of impact on the community is *Bent Bollywood*, a queer cabaret show exploring gender and sexuality. One thing that we tried to do in this work is to create a show that's really gay, really trans, really slutty, really sexual and is very informed by nightclub queer performance art, but also has a strong South Asianness about it. So it's got classical Indian dance; it draws on Hindu iconography and story and praxis.

We weren't sure how it would be received. But it was received amazingly. We didn't need to be nervous at all! We had really good critical responses, but more important to us was we had some incredible audience responses. People wrote to us, saying 'I'm South Asian and I'm queer and I cried watching the show because this was the first time that I felt hope that I could reconcile these two parts of my identity', which was really quite beautiful. That's what we were trying to achieve in the work. A lot of queer people of colour, we feel we have to compartmentalise our identity: we keep our gender and sexual identity separate from our cultural identities. But we were trying to show in this work that you can be queer and South Asian, and that's not a conflict. South Asians, we *invented* camp! We're like the campest people, the most fabulous people on the planet, you know? Being queer and South Asian is a cohesive whole identity and you can see this in front of you in this work.

Notes

1 Shepparton is a rural town in the north of the Australian state of Victoria. It is about 180 kilometres from the state capital of Melbourne. The other towns Sonya mentions subsequently (Echuca and Mooroopna) are nearby.

2 Gippsland is the Southeastern region of Victoria, and is among the most sparsely populated parts of the state.

3 The island of Tasmania is Australia's southernmost state, and is approximately 320 kilometres long and wide.

4 The long-running American animated TV series *The Simpsons* debuted in 1989, with the character Apu Nahasapeemapetilon, the Indian-American proprietor of the Kwik-E-Mart, first appearing in 1990. Apu's character has been widely criticised as a racial stereotype, and in 2020, the non-Indian actor Hank Azaria, who had voiced Apu since the character's inception, announced that he would no longer be doing so.

5 Diwali is the Hindu festival of lights.

6 A small town in Gippsland, Victoria.

7 A well-known Australian chain selling fabrics and sewing and handicraft equipment.

8 A South Indian classical dance form that is widely practiced among Indian diasporic communities.

9 A noted practitioner and teacher of two performance forms from the south Indian state of Kerala, Mohiniyattam and Kathakali, Tara Rajkumar established the Natya Sudha Dance Company and School in Melbourne in 1986. *Mahamaya* was performed in 1997. The Alexander Theatre is on the campus of Monash University, in the east of Melbourne.

10 A regional town east of Melbourne.

11 Ausdance is a body that supports and advocates for dance initiatives in Australia.

12 One of four selective entry government schools in Victoria.

13 Port Douglas is a small coastal town in the north of the Australian state of Queensland. The television show Sonya is referring to is *Ocean Girl*, which ran for four seasons, from 1994–1997.

14 During the 2013 election campaign, the right-wing Liberal National coalition placed significant emphasis on border security. They announced that they would 'stop the boats' – a reference to attempts by asylum seekers to enter Australian territory by boat from Indonesia. The Coalition won the election, and implemented a strict border control policy called Operation Sovereign Borders.

15 *Melbourne Talam* was written by Rashma N. Kalsi and directed by Petra Kalive for Melbourne Theatre Company, one of the largest mainstream theatre companies in Australia.

16 Victorian towns in, respectively, the far northwest and northeast corners of the state.

17 Born, respectively, in Malaysia and India, Dr Chandrabhanu and Padma Menon are two long-standing exponents of Bharatanatyam, Kuchipudi and other classical Indian dance forms in Australia, as well as noted innovators in the choreography of hybrid and multicultural dance. The Victorian Arts Centre is the original name for the city-centre complex of performing arts venues that is today known as Arts Centre Melbourne.

18 John Howard was Prime Minister of Australia from 1996–2007, and is widely viewed as having overseen a significant rightwards shift in the Australian political climate.

19 In 2019, the report 'Shifting the Balance', produced by Diversity Arts Australia, concluded that culturally and/or linguistically diverse (CALD) Australians were under-represented in all sectors of the cultural industries, and that performing arts was the worst-performing sector, where only 5% of leaders were CALD Australians, compared to 30% of the Australian population. See Diversity Arts Australia, BYP Group and Western Sydney University, 'Shifting the Balance: Cultural Diversity in Leadership within the Australian Arts, Screen and Creative Sectors' (Sydney: Diversity Arts Australia, 2019). Available at http://diversityarts.org.au/tools-resources/launch-report-culturally-diverse-arts-leadership/ (Accessed 20 May 2020).

20 *Hungry Ghosts* was by the Malaysia-born playwright Jean Tong, and *Golden Shield* by Thai-Australian Anchuli Felicia King.

21 Ceremonial Hindu worship.

3

Good Chance Theatre

Margins and main stages

Interviewed and transcribed by
Emma Cox

Link | https://www.digitaltheatreplus.com/education/
collections/digital-theatre/good-chance-theatre-
margins-and-main-stages-joe-murphy-joe

Part I: an interview with Joe Murphy and Joe Robertson

Origins: travelling to Calais

JOE MURPHY: We first began working in Calais [in 2015]; it was sort of an accident really. We had finished writing a play up in Manchester, we had a little bit of time, we had a few friends who had been to Calais to do some voluntary work there, and they said, 'why don't you come and help in some capacity?' We didn't really have any understanding of what the situation was there, what kinds of people were there, the reason for its existence, the camp. We had a little bit of time, so we went down and found this city, this place which was a congregation, a temporary place, for about 10,000 people, I'd say, around that time, does that sound about right, 10,000? [to Robertson]

DOI: 10.4324/9781003199755-3

JOE ROBERTSON: Yes, from about 25 different nationalities. The conditions were terrible. And just to put this in context, this was at the time – the height of the European 'refugee crisis' as it became known – when the TV programmes that we were watching and the news and the newspapers were full of images of people travelling. I don't know what we expected but certainly not the place that we found, which was in spite of the conditions quite developed, the people there had begun to build restaurants and shops and cafes, and there was even a sauna. There were churches and mosques, you know, places of community. Structures that enabled people to, I suppose, survive. We ended up staying for a week.

JM: With some Kuwaiti people that we met. And we spent a few days, about a week, I'd say, around a campfire, telling stories at night, and just listening, really, but [in] everyone that we met there was this need for expression, to talk about, if not journeys people had been on, then stories of home and memories.

JR: It was palpable, that need. People were … we'd shake their hands and before you'd even found out their name you were hearing about what was happening and where that person had come from, and in that atmosphere, I think that was very interesting for us as playwrights, because stories are so important and they help us understand where we are and where we're going. And so we thought, actually, how could we help? I'm not very good at building, certainly not very good at cooking. But I can do theatre, so we thought maybe if we build a theatre people could tell their stories together; that'd probably be quite useful. And that's what we did, about a week later.

On Good Chance as 'participatory' theatre

JM: To be honest, I don't really understand what that ['participatory'] means, as a separate thing from the word 'theatre'. All theatre is participatory to a degree, and all theatre,
I suppose, is therapeutic, to a degree. All of it, even above
that level, is provocative and challenging, and I think the
work that we did alongside all the people that came into
the theatre in Calais was just theatre, really, on a very
basic level.

JR: And theatre meaning, not just a play that starts at 7:30 in
the evening, but also clay model making, music, dance,
debate; it was as much a theatre as a town hall. We could
have called it an arts centre or, I suppose, a community
centre, but that word theatre, and I think what it means
for us – theatre's always been a place of safety for me, a
place of sanctuary, in a way, where I will be welcomed,
and I know that I won't be judged, I suppose. And that's,
I think, what very quickly happened in the theatre in
Calais. Everyone built it together; there were about 100
people on the day we built it, run by a young boy called
Siddiq from Sudan who had some building expertise, and
he sort of ran the show. And as soon as it was up, people
started performing together and it was more of a theatre
than I've ever been in, than any theatre, I think.

JM: I think that's the thing; that word 'theatre' comes with a
lot of packaging around it now, in Europe, there's a for-
malised version of what it is. And it means – like you say
[to Robertson] – to go in at 7:30 and to sit in your place,
and you're in a certain row and a certain number and
you've got a comfy seat, and all will be well and you'll
see this show that is put in front of you. There's a sort

of limit to your involvement. The theatre that existed in Calais, and the theatres that we've built since, in similar situations, are – they're *real* theatres. You don't have rows of seating, that's fluid, and it changes, and every audience member who comes into the theatre has the potential to be part of what the show becomes. It's fluid.

On artistic collision: tradition and innovation

JR: The people we met in Calais and continue to work with now, and people we're currently working with in Paris, who are recently arriving in France and in Europe, have come with these amazing artistic traditions, beautiful musical traditions, or traditions of dance or painting or poetry. And similarly we, I think, come with our own traditions. For my own part how I understand myself, I suppose, is that they're part of my own personal, collective narrative. I think without a place where I could express those I'd be unmoored from who I am or what I think. And in the theatre what happens is all these traditions can suddenly have a platform, in a place where it's really important for that to exist and to have expression. And then something else amazing happens when these traditions start to collide and these stars of performers start to come together, and you know, you have Afghan dance over a Sudanese djembe, and someone from Eritrea is singing, and suddenly the soprano from the French Opera comes, and you're going, 'what is this?', and this is all new, and there is something in that collision that is really powerful. And that, I think, is the biggest inspiration for me, when everyone feels it, in the space, and something new is happening.

JM: I definitely think that it showed us a picture of the world that we hadn't seen before. It showed the things that you [Robertson] describe, and it presented to us a way of taking that then outside the theatre, through the art that was made in the theatre. So for us as playwrights, we were suddenly beginning to get a little bit obsessed with poetry from other countries, and how to meld that into the kind of dialogue that we were writing, which has certainly been a huge influence on our approach to sitting in front of a piece of paper.

JR: I also think it's made me angry.

JM: Yeah.

JR: And aware of my own ignorance, to a huge degree. Ignorance of the situations and a lot of the places that people are coming from, and you know, ignorance of just how difficult that moment of welcome can be for people. And an anger about that. An anger that I think has really driven our own work and our own writing. There's a sense of activation about it.

On collaboration: the National Theatre and the Young Vic

JM: I think the play that we wrote, *The Jungle*, came about in quite a peculiar way. We were commissioned by the National Theatre, but then very quickly the Young Vic came on board as a co-producing partner, and also Good Chance, the company that builds the theatres and that we run. But we've always collaborated, and we've always sought to try to bring as many organisations and individuals into a project as possible. I think that's part of the philosophy, and we believe creates something that is ultimately more unified and more exciting.

JR: It's that collision thing again.

JM: Exactly.

JR: It's crazy that the National [Theatre] and the Young Vic hadn't worked together before, and they're 'round the corner. Suddenly you have everyone in a room and they're talking in different ways, and you have to create new ways of doing things. And exciting things happen when you're in that situation. But that initial – Rufus [Norris] and the National being involved – they'd come out [to Calais] themselves, and helped out. The [NT] Production Manager had come and built things and delivered an old set, all reused set that we'd got from a big warehouse and we used that for a floor. And everyone, at least in the theatre world, and further afield as well, sort of tried to help, and it's [a] coming together thing, people banding together and giving what they can and helping where they can. And Rufus came out and saw a couple of shows in Calais – the Artistic Director of the National, Rufus – that was how we, once we'd had the *idea* for the play, which didn't come until much later and there was no plan to really; the theatre was for people to tell their own stories, not for us to write anything. And when that idea did happen, that's how it sort of…

JM: And I will say that it's never an easy process, a co-producing, collaborative relationship, and we don't mean to portray it as something that was romantically, you know, drifted towards a beautiful end result and everything was fine. As with anything, you negotiate, and you work out where each person and each organisation is coming from, and that is why it's part of our philosophy as a company, because we're in a world that is moving, now, and whatever your political stance is on issues of migration or issues to do with Europe, we do face a situation where lots of different people with different traditions are side by side now.

JR: That's exactly right, it's what the play is.

JM: It has to be the role of art to allow introductions to happen, and to allow those negotiations to happen, so that we can live together more thoroughly, more hopefully and in a better way.

Staging The Jungle at the Young Vic

JM: I remember when we first sat down and had made the decision and had spoken to the National about the possibility of writing *The Jungle*. We sat down together and thought, how do we want this play to feel? How does it have to feel based on the experiences that we had and that we saw many people go through? We decided that it had to be a very fluid experience, that the audience would have, and that, somehow, we had to find a way for the audience to be *within* the Jungle. But at the same time, the Jungle was quite a big place, and it was quite… there were lots of little centres to it. So how do you specifically position the audience within a place in the Jungle that somehow speaks of the Jungle at large. That's how we came to this idea of the restaurant, because it was a centre for people of many different nationalities. It was run by an Afghan, but it was visited by Somalians, Sudanese people, Eritreans, so it felt like a hub, and a hub that the audience could be part of.

JR: Those structures in the Jungle were places of sanctuary. They were places of community, where people ate together and drank chai tea together. There was a big fire, which often happened; people would go to them, and when it was raining and freezing and cold, that's where you'd go and get some hot nan bread that had just been cooked. And that seemed to also get at the heart of what the play is about, because it's within that chaos, within the crisis, and the conditions, and the difficulty, of lots of different people literally on top of each other, it's the structures that we have to make and that we do make and that people did make in the Jungle, that are made to help you and the community at large get through that situation. Those structures were so important in the Jungle, and I think the play is about how people live together – on top of each other, from different places, from different cultures, from radically different perspectives. And it's the struggle of coming together, and that's what happened in those restaurants. And it's not one restaurant, it's sort of an amalgamation of lots of different places, and there's a bit of our theatre in there as well, I think.

JM: Yes.

JR: Lots of meetings that happened, community meetings. I think the audience, the experience with the audience, it's like this, actually [gestures to the low couch he is sitting on], everyone had to lean forward because they were on benches, and they were desperately uncomfortable, but I think anyone expecting to be able to sit down and relax were probably surprised that you had to learn forward; there was a different kind of experience of being in that place. We struggled with the word 'immersive', you know, immersive, you're given things and you have to do things and it's all very stressful, but people got nan bread if they wanted it, and some chai tea, and you were really in that meeting, you were really in that community meeting, or that moment in the restaurant.

JM: It's back to what we were talking about earlier with the theatre in Calais, of what is asked of an audience when they enter a theatre, it's just [that] the relationship between the audience that came to see *The Jungle* and the Jungle was altered inasmuch as they had to lean forward, as you [Robertson] described; they had an experience or a level of comfort that they don't normally associate with a theatre, that is more applicable to how they imagine that restaurant in the Jungle *really* was.

JR: It was very intimate, you know, things happened all around you, suddenly there was someone behind you …

JM: We wanted things to crash into each other.

JR: You had to move your legs if there was an actor running by.

JM: We didn't want people to be able to [leans back and folds arms over chest] …

JR: You're out of focus now. See, exactly.

JM: … [laughs] to do that. That felt like the wrong thing to aim for and it would have been, to a degree, insincere and unrepresentative of the struggles that many, many people faced in that place.

JR: And people are still – there's 1,000 people in Calais now. We didn't want anyone to go in and sit and enjoy a lovely play, you know. It provokes people, it's not always comfortable. It [the Calais Jungle] was often very funny, with music happening all around, but we wanted to make that … You know, you'd walk into the Jungle, there'd be so many people talking to you, you never finished a conversation. There was always something terrible happening, or a crisis, or a teargas canister landing next to you, or a riot, and it's important that that was represented and the [Young Vic] space allowed that.

Continuing relationships: working with refugee artists

JR: In the play, there were three actors who we'd met in the Jungle, who we worked with in the dome, in the theatre, [as well as] fantastic musicians, a brilliant circus performer, and it was amazing being able to continue working with them. They'd arrived in Britain, but obviously throughout the seven months we lived in Calais, we met many, many fantastic artists and performers and people who may not have been artists where they came from but who were creatively activated by their journey. People like Misba, a brilliant Afghan man, a very young man, with nine brothers and sisters, I think, who were all with him and he was a sort of patriarch, really, in that situation. And he was deaf, and couldn't speak but could use his body and his face to tell the most amazing stories, that would last 45 minutes, and the theatre would be full of 300 people just sitting in silence on a night – the heater's on and it's cold outside – and he's telling this story through mime that is his journey from Afghanistan, and arriving in the Jungle, his hope for the future. And I remember the day he left the Jungle, and that was a decision not to continue to try to cross the border every night, but to go to Sweden. But there are so many people. Siddiq who built the theatre and is now in Brittany, and he would sing every night in our hope shows that we had in the evening. Brilliant people who it would be amazing to continue to work with. We've seen a couple of them in Paris and in France.

JM: But this is a reality for many people is that you can't always make choices, I suppose, in your life. And there are people, great artists that you've talked about [to Robertson] that are living in different places across Europe now and we'd love to be able to continue working with them in this, which is why the work in Paris that we're doing at the moment – where we have a theatre up in the north east of the city – is so important, because it gives us the possibility of continuing relationships and creating more work. So if people can't have a relationship with *The Jungle* per se, they can have a contribution to something new, that speaks to their situation right now. The experience of the play, *The Jungle*, will not be a summation of the experience of many people, even those who lived in the Jungle. It's just one thing. And we hope that Good Chance can continue to make things that create more perspectives for more people.

JR: And that, crucially, will enable people who've worked in the space to have a new language to be able to do that themselves. I know lots of people who've worked in the space who've gone to different places and have carried on their artistic work in different countries, and that's the amazing thing. That's, I think, that's how it can continue when the dome disappears. Because the dome will always, in the end, disappear.

Beyond the camp: the Paris project

JR: We have been working in Paris for the last three months. We built our dome in Paris's largest refugee and migrant welcome centre, in Port de la Chappelle, which is in the north, just inside the [Boulevard] Périphérique. The centre is the first port of call for people when they arrive in the city. You often stay on the streets for several months before you can get into that centre, you stay in the centre for a few weeks and then are moved to another centre around France, if you enter the asylum process. And we built our dome – two domes, a big dome and a petit dome – inside the centre. The main aim of that project, and the main aim of our work with Good Chance now, is sort of beyond the situation of a camp like Calais, where it was an immensely critical crisis situation. People had just arrived. But now I think the challenge is how European cities, big cities – like Paris, like London – how they welcome people who are arriving. And how we create spaces of welcome in really busy, really densely populated places, these urban areas – that have their own problems, and their own difficulties – especially places like Port de la Chappelle. How do we create that welcome in cities? That's the big challenge. That's what we've been trying to do in Paris. Bringing newly arrived people together with local artists, local volunteers, and trying to create work through art. It's been an amazing couple of months.

JM: I think that's right; the work in Calais was reactionary, it was instinctive, it was – like you say [to Robertson] – it was an emergency. Now, the work that we're doing, we're trying a little bit more to build an idea of how to use art to make introductions between people who've just arrived in a city and those who've lived there all their lives. And using art as a go-between, as a 'hello' at the start of a conversation. Because how would you meet somebody who's just arrived in a city? It's a really difficult thing; often cities are very atomised. And we think that art is a very important tool for the beginning of that conversation.

JR: The really open civic spaces in our cities are disappearing, and where do you have permission to meet another person, where? And theatre's got to stake its claim in that respect and intervene in moments like this, where tensions are really forming. I'm from Hull and I grew up with an awareness of this in Hull. Same with you [to Murphy] in Leeds, and it's the same now. Like it or not, this subject is really controversial, and it's really contentious for a lot of people, and a lot of people with their own problems. So I think we've got a role as artists to intervene and say, 'okay, let's try and get together, let's try and understand each other'. If you sit in front of someone reading a poem, suddenly you're disarmed a bit, and you can view someone as a person, I think.

JM: Which might sound flighty and romantic, but –

JR: It's really solid, it's concrete.

JM: It is. It's actually, when you enter one of the places that we're talking about or the theatres that we build, it's a grounded experience. It's not a concept. It's being like that [moves across shoulder to shoulder with Robertson] right next to somebody who you've never met before and you're watching something that might be in another language or it might be – like you say [gestures to Robertson] – it might be mime, and it might be a Mr Bean sketch that we had this Saturday just gone [laughs].

JR: Yes, so we have these weekly hope shows, and the hope shows are the days that we literally open the doors to everyone in Paris and we've had people from loads of different areas of French society coming in and sitting, and they're going, 'what is this?' And they leave going, 'wow, what is this?' And even a little thing, like this chap from Afghanistan, he stood up, and it was his turn in the show, and no-one knew what he was going to do and he said, 'can you all do this' [crosses arms and fingers, touches the sides of each nostril, lifts elbows up]. I can't do it as well as him.

JM: And everyone was going [tries the trick, feigns confusion].

JR: And you're going, what's the purpose, and that might sound flighty and romantic and silly, but in that moment, the connection between everyone in the room was *so* strong.

JM: I'm really impressed that you can do it, by the way.

West End transfer: diversifying audiences

JM: I think as *The Jungle* transfers into the West End – which is really exciting – I think one of the big challenges for us is to allow the doors of the theatre to be really open, to remain as open as they were at the Young Vic – which has the most fantastic outreach department.

JR: Diverse audiences.

JM: Diverse audiences. They do so much work for the productions and it's a natural process for them and they're just brilliant at it. The West End, not so brilliant. And so, we're really proud, for example, that we've got one of the most radical ticketing schemes that will hopefully welcome people from all different classes, different political opinions, as well. We have 40% of tickets that are below £25, which is just a real massive step forward and we've had conversations with people going, 'how have you done that?' who've been really excited about that.

JR: I think we never, really ... for us *The Jungle* piece was always going to be this small, intimate show, with our friends from Calais and lots of friends who we've worked with since, and we're really overwhelmed by the response, and by how much connection there was between the audience and the performance and the stories. And I think it was because, for so many – the actors and for us, and for lots of people involved – it was really personally important. And that integrity is so vital and I think maintaining that in a huge, one of the beautiful theatres of London, maintaining that integrity, and also that intimacy that we talked about, maintaining that in that bigger space will be really important. So the design has had to be radically redesigned; we've tried to adapt the space to the design, rather than trying to change the design to fit the space. So we're doing something quite amazing, we're boarding over everything, and creating the Afghan restaurant out of the infrastructure and the kind of architecture of the theatre. And of course, you know, it's all Italianate, you've got this big cross arch and suddenly you've got to suck in in the middle. And so we've had to figure out how that can work. But all those discussions are exciting. I think when people left the Young Vic show, everyone said 'what can I do, what can I do?' And being able to be in the West End, a stone's throw from Parliament, in the centre of the theatrical discourse, right in the middle, and going, 'this deserves to be on the stage', and then utilising that. When people come out with that same instinct, 'what do I do, what do I do?' we're trying to give people options. So we're working with refugees, some of our other friends to go, okay, what can you do, how can you find out more, how can you take that sort of determination to put it into action, I suppose.

JM: There's also an important part of us that wants this to act as the beginning of a discussion. We never wanted the play to, for it to have the possibility to be simplified. To, for example, be an argument to open the borders, for everyone, and that's the end of the discussion and you can go out and you know what the message of the playwrights is. That's not what we want. We want it to be quite a complicated beginning. So that people who are of a different political opinion to the one that I've just described can feel as welcome in that space as those people [that agree with it]. And there's a real question between those [differing opinions]. And I think it will be really interesting, as we move from the Young Vic into the West End, what kinds of people we get, because it will be a different audience. Perhaps we will encounter more people who are not as naturally sympathetic to the argument that I described about borders.

JR: It's really important, that, really important.

JM: It is.

JR: And it's not easy, as well, to welcome people who wouldn't necessarily go to theatre or who wouldn't take this kind of interest in the subject matter; but how we try and talk about this and how we market it, they're all really important tools for creating a discussion that should happen but that isn't happening in the right way at the moment.

Part 2: a conversation with Joe Murphy, Joe Robertson and Majid Adin

JR: Hello Majid.

JM: Nice to see you again.

MAJID ADIN: Nice to see you too.

JR: I was just thinking back to when we first met in the Jungle. It feels like a very long time ago.

MA: I arrived to Calais, early November 2015, but I found Good Chance Theatre after two or three weeks, I think, late November.

JM: It was a rainy day, I remember, it was not a nice day.

MA: I remember I couldn't find Good Chance Theatre, and for two or three weeks I was in the Jungle. I told you I was looking for the distribution centre – I was looking for shoes! – and I find Good Chance Theatre. The building, the dome, it was a very interesting, place, with the tent of the dome.

JR: There definitely weren't any shoes.

MA: I was upset that I couldn't find it [laughs].

JM: [laughs] no we didn't have shoes, or coats, or anything useful.

JR: It was sort of deliberate. I mean it was – there were lots of other places in the Jungle where you could get these things, not enough, but it felt important that there was this space where it wasn't about what … it was about something else, it was about a choice, a choice to go there. Does that make sense?

JM: We talked about this, that it's not something that you need, it's something that you want. And because you really want it, you sort of need it, if that makes sense.

MA: I never thought about art; I never thought about looking for places in the Jungle for art. It was very different. At that time, life in the Jungle, for me, it was, the shape of life, it was a very primitive life. Like primitive humans, you're waking up and hunting, finding something, wake up in the morning and looking for some places for distribution centre, some clothes or some food.

JR: But then you did come back to the dome and you said, I remember you running in and saying 'I need a paintbrush'.

MA: Yes, in the morning; I can't remember exactly what time, it was noon or morning, I met the first person, Amy. I remember the shape of the dome – it was spiritual, for me, because it was a big dome – I thought, 'what's that?' like it came from another planet, 'what's that, this tent, what is this part of the Jungle?' The distribution centre, they give something – clothes, shoes – and I remember, I came inside [the dome], it was not too crowded. Some people, they did play, and I came and I sat in the corner and thought, 'what are they doing in the Jungle?' I couldn't find the shoes, clothes anything! What's that?! But, I don't know, [after] ten minutes, 15 minutes, Amy came to me and [asked] me, 'you want to do a painting, or something?' For many years, I'd never painted. I thought, 'mmm, I don't know; yes'. I began with some paper and markers, colour or something. And I painted something, and then I left the dome. And I came back again in the evening again.

JM: Which is when we had all our shows.

MA: I remember that. My feeling is the connection to the dome. It's very emotional for me. After one day or two days, I came back, it was evening or night. That time it was very crowded. I remember the next person I met was Joe [touches Robertson's knee]. I think four or five groups, small groups, they were acting, a play or something. In the corner, they invited some refugees. In one group, there were some beautiful girls, in that group [gestures distance], acting or something, and I wanted to go to that group. Joe [Robertson] told me 'hey, come to my group!' [laughs]

JR: I'm so sorry [laughs].

MA: I wanted to go to that other group. [laughs] But I came to your group, it was four or five persons. And I had never acted in all my life.

JR: Really?

MA: I'm untalented at acting because I'm a very shy person. That time, if you remember, me and you were acting something, we were sitting…

JR: Were we in a school? Was it a school scene, or?

MA: No, it was very short, five minutes, two minutes… My first acting of my life, it was with you.

JR: And you you're – you've carried on the acting [laughs]. We would do all these improvisations in the Jungle, and it was amazing. I suppose you'd expect them all to be – I don't know what you'd expect them to be – but I was blown away by how many of the improvisations were in schools, or in meetings.

MA: I don't know what you mean by 'improvisation'.

JM: It's when you make up something, so if we were to sit here now and pretend to be somebody else but we didn't have the words. We would be improvising.

JR: You'd just make up the story.

MA: Ah, yes, yes.

JR: People would always say, 'let's set it in a school, or in a hospital, or in a meeting room'.

JM: It's interesting what people remember about where they come from and where people *want* to remember.

JR: There were these structures.

JM: Places that people understood, like you say [to Robertson], a school or a mosque or a hospital or places like this.

JR: Sort of safe. I thought that was interesting.

MA: One thing that was very interesting for me was, because normally – and I don't want to say racist or looking down or something – but I felt, and it's maybe not that positive to say, but I felt that when somebody came to the Jungle, some European, western people, they'd be looking down to us. Too kind, not unkind, too much kind, but looking to us as uncivilised persons. In the dome – because it was the first for me, when I came to the dome – I did painting or art or something. I said, yes, 'I can paint, I can do art' – you don't need to be kind or not kind. It gave me a very good feeling: 'yes, I have a culture, I can paint. I can do anything, I am civilised.' That gave me a very good feeling.

JM: Do you know what, I think that's such an important point because I think [for] a lot of people from all over the world there is an idea of charity, and the person who has power and money comes to help other people, and those people are down here, and without the help of this person that other person will always struggle. But we tried to get rid of that idea, I think, in the dome, to varying degrees of success.

JR: You know, all the volunteers were kind, of course. In a way, trying to get a dome to do what it [is] we do was in response to that. I think sometimes charity can be a one-way street. There were some volunteers who really didn't want refugees involved in the distribution process, or this kind of process. But the thing about art is it really can happen on an equal basis, whether you're acting together or painting.

JM: Yes, and the best art depends upon lots of different people. It's always getting ideas off each other and then going away and thinking and then having another conversation. You're always making things with other people.

MA: I remember one time in the corner of the dome I was painting something. And one person came and said something like, 'oh, you can paint', like [I was a] primitive person, never known about art, like 'oh that's very beautiful, you can paint', like that. She was a French person [laughs]. Not about the French-English thing, but I said, 'I know', and I said names of a lot of names of French painters; I know this better than you! 'I know Charles Baudelaire, I love Baudelaire poems', but I'd read one poem of Baudelaire's! Not too much. I said, 'I know the culture more than you'.

JR: You should have shown them your degree in Fine Art from Tehran University [laughs].

MA: This feeling [at the dome], it makes a very good feeling. We know we can make art.

JR: You became, you *were*, one of the central people in the dome for the time that you were in the Jungle. As well as painting every day, you also designed sets for the some of the big shows that we put on. I remember on Yalda night [Iranian winter solstice], remember you organised Yalda night, which was a big celebration, and we watched an Iranian film and you did that huge board, which we've still got, celebrating Yalda night. You became part of the DNA of Good Chance.

MA: Yes. And about the acting, plays, music, etc., it was like a university for me. I went to the Arts University in Iran. But we lived in an Islamic country and the Arts University is completely controlled by Islamic rule. It's closed, we didn't have an art or music university department. When I came to the dome, theatre was completely new for me. I didn't know anything. Maybe all of my life before that, maybe ten times, or something, I'd watched a play or something. It was so interesting because the different groups who came to the dome had different techniques, different doings. I loved sitting in the corner and analysing, thinking, 'this is what they do'. Because I realise that something they did in their play or acting is like painting because it's visualised. I thought, 'this is how they work in this space with the imagination of the people'. How to make the creation of the imagination. I watched them and analysed, and for me it was very interesting and very new, completely.

JM: Did you notice, did your painting change? Or your idea of painting and design change as you went through the Jungle? Can you describe that?

MA: It did change. Normally when I was in Iran, when I was a student, I never used water colour. Normally I painted in oil or acrylic. Maybe there were some things that I found in the dome, some ink or some watercolour, I don't know why, but because of this material, and because my mood had changed at that time. The material changed and the atmosphere of the paintings [changed]. The moment in my painting, representing that moment, yes, it was more poetic than before. A different atmosphere.

JM: When I think of your paintings, I always think about the way that you use colour. They're not bright colours, they're hopeful, they're optimistic, but they're slightly faded in a way as well, and I think, for a lot of people, they imagine that somebody who is living in a difficult place and it's a difficult time in their lives, perhaps they wouldn't paint in this way. But you were creating things that were hopeful.

MA: That's a psychological complexity. I had a big gap, about a ten-year gap, between my last paintings, and these paintings. That period of my life, that gap, my perspective and looking to the world changed. At that time [at university], I'm looking to the world and I thought, 'yes, I can do anything', my looking to life it was, 'you can make, you can manage your life, exactly [as] you think'. This period of ten years [since], anything has happened for me. I don't know what happened, [I was] just following the life; I don't know what happened for me. And I found this atmosphere in the watercolour. I don't know tomorrow or next year what [will] happen to me. I decided, in the watercolour, [to] express some colour. After that I decided what can I paint and how can I paint. I came to the painting step by step, I never thought about managing before that. Because now also, I don't know what happened, I just need a match with life. It's a difficult thing to say in English. Maybe one is the watercolour and one is a monochromatic. The colour, a bit, is sadness. Now also in my painting I don't decide, 'what can I paint?' I prefer the painting to say to me what can I paint. I just follow the task. This is now my viewing on life. Exactly, I can't say, because many things have happened to me, negative. I couldn't decide what happened, what can I be.

JM: It's exactly the same, I think, with us. There'll never be a point when we'll sit down and go, 'now we will start this play, and it will be about this thing'. You can't define that moment. The play has already started. And there will be a moment where it begins to get written. When you arrived in Britain, you continued painting and making and using art. One of the ways that you kept doing that was through animation.

MA: Yes.

JR: Yes, because you said in the Jungle, we said 'when you get to Britain do you want to be a painter' and you said 'no, I want to be an animator'. We were like 'oooh'.

MA: I never thought you could be an animator so soon in the UK [laughs].

JR: We actually talked about it. When we had a meeting in your caravan, because there was a film being made about Good Chance and you were going to do an animated section. And then the Jungle got evicted and it all went a bit chaotic.

MA: I think the first time I met you [pointing at Murphy] we talked animation or something. Amy introduced me to you, and we spoke about animation.

JM: I remember. It was a very quick thing, and then, when you arrived here, it's even quicker, because suddenly...

JR: You're now a major animator.

JM: You're a brilliant animator.

MA: I never thought that I could very soon be an animator. In the Jungle I asked someone, 'if I came to the UK, can I be an animator?' And I guessed from the face that it was 'you can... (but you cannot!)'.

JR: Yeah, 'good luck with that, good luck'.

MA: Yes, good luck! But yes, I did *Rocket Man*. I think, *Rocket Man*, it doesn't happen [often], really, I didn't think ever, at all, that I could find work as an animator here. *Rocket Man* was like a miracle. But really, it was a good chance from Good Chance.

JM: It was a good chance.

JR: Yes. There was a competition to make a music video for [Elton John's] *Rocket Man*. I remember that meeting we had around the kitchen table [in the UK]. It was quite random, we were just having dinner or something, later

on, and I went 'oh, I saw this competition', and we just
started talking about it. And we listened to the song, and
just got talking about the character in the song is kind
of like people we met in Calais, the journey and leaving
home and being on Mars, it feels like. And you went away,
and you were like, 'well, maybe we'll do a treatment'. The
next day, it was fully made, this treatment video!

MA: You know, I came to your house, for a party or something, completely unrelated. You know, that was a very
important conversation, a very important conversation!
[laughs] I thought it was a competition for refugees from
the Jungle, or something, I never thought it was a big
competition, for anybody.

JM: It was a global competition, and your video will be seen
by 12 million!

MA: If I had known that, I never would have joined to do that.

JR: No.

MA: No, really! Because I never thought I could.

JR: Downplay, downplay. But it was, like, a day or two, and
then you came back with the treatment, just drawn
in pencil. And we just sat [looks shocked], and it was
one of those moments when you see something really
important.

JM: I watched it the other day [shakes head in admiration].

JR: It was so beautiful, that first treatment. And what you
eventually made, was beautiful, of course, but that first
treatment…

MA: You helped me, you told me and gave me some advice to
find a good view about the design, [and] that completely
helped. But it was like a miracle of God. Sometimes in
your life, as I say, you are at the right time and you are in
the right place. I think exactly this for *Rocket Man*.

JR: But also, you're a fantastic artist, your art speaks for itself. And I really think, you won the competition, but had you not, you would still be able to do – now you're making lots of films.

JM: I don't know why I ask this, but do you just call yourself an artist, or do you call yourself an artist who is a refugee, or a refugee artist, or an artist who paints about the experience of being a refugee?

MA: I think I can say artist. For example, would you say, you are an English artist, and Londoner artist, no it's not this adjective. Yes, I am a refugee for a different situation, and of course, being a refugee is some part of my life. For example, I am a man, I am born in Iran, many situations. If you are a real artist, your art is influenced by all of the situations of your life – nationality, situation, all of it. Your art is influenced by all of them. I am an artist and also a refugee.

JM: Well, thank you.

JR: Thank you very, very much. It's lovely to talk to you, Majid.

MA: Thank you very much.

4

The heat signatures of refugee transit

Incoming by Richard Mosse

Emma Cox

Link | https://www.digitaltheatreplus.com/education/
collections/digital-theatre/the-heat-signatures-of-
refugee-transit-incoming-by-richard

How might artists play a role in shaping responses to one of
our era's greatest challenges, that of unprecedented refugee
movement? And how might the representation of refugees
in the arts prompt awareness of how human movement is
interlocked with larger global systems and flows? In seeking
to answer these questions, I want to pursue a key idea: that it
is increasingly necessary to understand refugee crises hand in
hand with *both* global climate change *and* with military engagement. Climate crisis is, of course, a major driver of forced
migration in our era, as agricultural lands are destroyed, while
the sophisticated coercive technologies used to respond to
refugees overlap with military technologies. I will orient this
discussion around an artistic work that weaves these threads
together. *Incoming*[1] by Irish photographer Richard Mosse is a
52-minute, three-channel video installation co-commissioned
by London's Barbican and Melbourne's National Gallery of
Victoria. First shown at the Barbican at the start of 2017, it has

DOI: 10.4324/9781003199755-4

since been presented at major galleries including the National Gallery of Victoria, Melbourne (2017–2018), the Bunkier Sztuki Gallery of Contemporary Art, Kraków (2019), le Lieu Unique, Nantes (2019), the Institute of Contemporary Art, Boston (2019), the San Francisco Museum of Modern Art (2019–2020), and the National Gallery of Art, Washington DC (2019).

Co-created with cinematographer Trevor Tweeten and composer Ben Frost, *Incoming* comprises slow motion cinematography and stills, taken between 2014 and 2017, of the 'refugee crisis' in Europe: sea rescues, ferry transportation and footage from refugee camps in Greece, France, Italy and Germany. But it also draws on a wider field, with images of a people smugglers' transit hub in the Sahara, of military operations launched from a US aircraft carrier in the Persian Gulf, and of airstrikes in northern Syria, viewed from across the Turkish border. Semi-abstract shots are interspersed, of a lunar landscape, ocean surfaces and a dawn sky. The images are projected onto three eight-metre-wide screens.

While the footage that makes up *Incoming* comes from sites in the northern hemisphere (the Persian Gulf, the Sahara and Europe), Mosse's work is contextually linked to Australia, both as a co-commission with a Melbourne gallery, and in terms of activism. When Mosse presented the work at Melbourne's National Gallery of Victoria, he proffered a critique of Australia's notorious refugee detention system, joining other artists in protesting the gallery's contract with Wilson Security, a former corporate security provider for Australia's offshore detention centres on Manus Island and Nauru. Mosse incorporated text and voice message into the installation from prominent Manus Island detainee, the Iranian journalist, filmmaker and activist Behrouz Boochani, stating, 'It is not acceptable that an art organisation like NGV has signed a contract with a company whose hands are so bloody.' By February 2018, the National Gallery of Victoria had cancelled its contract with Wilson Security.

Incoming enters what Mosse acknowledges is 'over-photographed' terrain. Photojournalism by outlets like AP, Getty and Reuters, as well as image-making by individuals on their smartphones, has contributed to making refugee movement, particularly across Europe, an intensely visual domain. But *Incoming* isn't a photographic work in the strict sense. Instead of registering particles of matter on the visible light spectrum, the camera detects heat signatures, representing people and objects in alarming close-up and from distances of over 30 kilometres. Unlike the rainbow spectrum of heat sensing imagery that we're more familiar with, this medium-wave infrared technology renders images in fine gradations of monochrome. So, the spectator is accessing data with the eyes that normally can only be *felt* with the sense of touch.

This distilling of bodies as metabolic signifiers points to the readiness with which refugee transit is collapsed into biological metaphors (whereby refugees are imagined as contaminants, parasites or things that nations need to in-oculate against). But *Incoming* also speaks to the reach of biometrics – which include Mosse's heat-sensitised images, as well as retina scans, fingerprints, facial maps and full-body scans – all confirming that biological and political systems are not just comparable, but enmeshed. The flick-ering contours of human metabolism are rendered as waxy faces, bleached hair and deep, gaping eye sockets. Together with the military and surveillance technologies that are shot through its videography, *Incoming* maps out a symp-tomology of violent system dysfunction. So it is perhaps less helpful to read this work as being 'about' refugees, or 'about' military engagement, or even climatic crisis, but rather, to recognise the ways that it shows us lines of connection between these signs of a global system under strain.

Incoming is the product of Mosse's repurposing of military-grade equipment. The thermographic camera, manufactured in the UK for a multinational weapons corporation, is meant for long-range battlefield awareness and border surveillance and is classified as a weapon, with its use controlled under International Traffic in Arms Regulations. Mosse points out that the camera 'was not designed for storytelling and was never intended to be used aesthetically' ('Richard Mosse's *Incoming*' 2017), and in the Barbican exhibition note and elsewhere he refers to using the technology 'against itself' to comment on how governments 'represent' and 'regard' the refugee. Certainly, thermographic cameras are objects that show up very clearly the continuities between military and border-control technologies: for example, EU nations now provision local authorities across North Africa with equipment, including thermal imaging cameras, to detect and stop migrants who would seek to enter the EU. This is what's called the 'externalising' of EU borders, and it's part of the same continuum between the arms, border control and security industries that Mosse and others protested in the context of Wilson Security's relationship with the NGV Melbourne.

A similar continuum is at play in Mosse's repurposing of the camera: while *Incoming* provokes reflections on the relationship between who is seen and who does the seeing, Mosse's imagery never lets us forget that the tool he is using originates with an invasive and destructive purpose. In this sense, *Incoming* might be understood as attaching itself to an image-saturated field that is already the means by which most of us relate to the military-industrial complex – or what has more recently been called the 'military-entertainment complex' (Caldwell and Lenoir 2017).

One way of comprehending how Mosse's work interlocks with such massive entities as the global military and security complexes is via philosopher Timothy Morton's concept of 'hyperobjects'. These, Morton argues, are 'things that are massively distributed in time and space relative to humans' (2013, 1), and as such difficult to comprehend as 'things' at all. In his book *Hyperobjects*, Morton situates global warming within this paradigm. I think that we can understand *Incoming* as a work that envisions the interlinked hyperobjects of global refugee crises, global warming and the military-industrial (or entertainment) complex. To put it another way, *Incoming* situates refugees *in and of* the Anthropocene (that is, the era of human-induced global transformation).

Part of how Mosse's camera envisions hyperobjects is by oscillating between vast and intimate scales. Faces, hands, implements and objects are rendered in intense close up, while panoramic shots from long distances scan territories horizontally in a mode reminiscent of military scoping. The viewer is afforded this dominant scoping view of an ISIS target as it comes under attack by a US missile; of an oceanscape as it is carved in an aircraft carrier's wake; and of refugees sitting in rows on the Greek island of Lesvos, awaiting processing. In another sequence, a long shot of a lunar surface zooms closer and closer until flickering heat transfers upon the alien topography move into view (this image putting the viewer in mind of other orbital bodies – the satellite infrastructures that have enabled humans to scope the entire planet).

Ben Frost's eight-channel soundtrack is similarly interested in the vast and intimate; it combines diegetic sound
from field recordings and non-diegetic, synthetic sound –
some of it high pitched, dissonant, metallic and uncomfortable. In a section shot from aboard a nuclear-powered aircraft
carrier, the USS Theodore Roosevelt, during airstrikes on
ISIS targets in Iraq and Syria, visual perception is gradually
superseded by auditory perception. US Airforce personnel
shoulder missiles, carrying them to trailers for transport
to the launch site. As the aircraft prepares for take-off, the
bass is so loud and deep it becomes all-encompassing. The
volume increases and the soundscape shifts from diegetic
sound to synthetic bass. This produces a visceral sensation
of low frequency 'tactile sound' that vibrates through the
gallery floor, walls and chairs and into the spectator's body,
hinting at the permeability of our fragile human tissue.

In their book *Research Theatre, Climate Change, and the
Ecocide Project: A Casebook*, Una Chaudhuri and Shonni
Enelow argue:

> The first thing that makes climate change difficult to rep-
> resent in art is the maddening fact that climate – unlike
> weather – can never be directly experienced. As the ag-
> gregation of numerous atmospheric and weather phe-
> nomena, climate does not manifest itself in any single
> moment, even, or location. The only way it can be appre-
> hended is through data and modeling – through systems
> and mediations – all of which have to be processed cog-
> nitively and intellectually.
>
> (Chaudhuri and Enelow 2014, 23)

Mosse recognises this challenge of apprehension via art, and
explains his hope that in *Incoming*, the 'idea of heat, imaging

heat [...] would speak sideways about human displacement resulting from climate change and global warming' (Mosse 2017). Similar representational dilemmas exist in the context of *en masse* refugee movement, and Mosse observes that the capabilities of the thermographic camera might allow new kinds of regard for other humans: *Incoming*, he says, enters 'an invisible spectrum of light in order to help people see again' ('Is Your Perception' 2017).

The installation also addresses the challenge of representing what is a crisis of aggregation (to use Chaudhuri and Enelow's language) by juxtaposing large, systemic scales and intimate, human scales, showing – and potentially enabling us to *sense* – how the one is inextricably intertwined with the other. *Incoming* does this by more than mere juxtaposition, however; the very means by which we see the work – i.e. via heat exchange – puts the micro or small into a macro or large context; we perceive small things and large as having impacts, altering environments, *doing* things in the world. Beyond its obvious references to refugee arrival, and to missile technology, the verb-form title of the piece, *Incoming*, suggests doings: transfers, processes and exchanges within a system. As a thermographic instrument, the camera sees shifts of temperature; it sees the products of the thermal motion of charged particles. Spectators of *Incoming* are, therefore, not looking at the materiality of human bodies, first and foremost, but at what they are *doing*.

In one sequence, an attempted rewarming of a refugee's body is performed on the northern coast of Lesvos following a sea rescue. As warm hands press into the hypothermic body, which is covered by a thermal blanket, black imprints appear where the relative heat leaves its trace. Mosse has noted that these images were taken at night, though there is no way of telling from the images themselves.

Simultaneously, on the right-hand screen, black handprints appear as refugees scramble off a dinghy; these marks on cold rubber visually echo those on the cold body, connecting the fading residues left at points of contact between humans, and between humans and objects.

Importantly, while human life clamours in *Incoming*, it is not thriving life. And the only living things we see other than humans are the occasional bird and a dog. Life exists within heavy industry: large ferries, trucks, train stations, shipping containers, a fighter jet, a helicopter, the concrete slabs of a refugee camp. These are framed by water and fire imagery, dual elements that serve as something like ecological touchstones in Mosse's vision. Surfaces of water appear viscous and oily. Fire rages during the forced dismantling of the 'Jungle' at Calais, France, after refugees and volunteers set parts of the camp alight in protest. The sequences depicting the burning of the Jungle hint at the eschatological (the idea of 'end times'); white hot flames reflect off firefighters' helmets as worshippers pray at a makeshift Eritrean Christian church, crucifixes cut into its prefab gate. Heat signatures from hands and faces are imprinted on the gate after prayers, before the church is burned. All this appears in slow motion, which seems to dilate time and call for a concentrated looking.

In his exhibition note, Mosse cites philosopher Giorgio Agamben's concept of bare life as a reference point. Agamben is a common touchstone in artistic and philosophical discussions of refugeehood, and while the foregrounding in *Incoming* of the camp and the noncitizen clearly situates the work as one that might be illuminated via Agamben, I think something subtly different is emerging in and through these thermodynamic images. Bare life, for Agamben, describes life that is held outside political categories: '*Life that cannot be sacrificed and yet may be killed*' (1998, 82, italics in original). As I have suggested, Mosse's camera sees bodies as 'doings', before it sees them as 'beings' (in the sense of identity, political status, rights – or lack thereof). People are imaged as nodes of heat energy that are affected by, and have effects upon, the spaces in which they move and dwell. In this view, we see natural laws first, political laws second.

The work's visualisation of heat transfers also provokes awareness of a networked, technologised environment, in which humans and machines interface constantly. In one sequence, a child at a refugee camp stares into a mobile phone, whose white glow seems to be reflected on her face and hands as she clutches the device with both hands. This is an illusion, of course: the white heat signatures are generated by her body's metabolism. But the image situates the mobile phone as talismanic. It serves as a reminder that in tandem with the increased sophistication of state surveillance and military engagement is the rise to ubiquity of smartphones, whose satellite navigation technologies (all military in origin) are crucial for facilitating refugees' mapping and communication. The totalising way in which location-based services have been integrated into civilian mapping can make it easy to forget that unauthorised transit is almost never, *technologically* speaking, clandestine. It is digitally networked; indeed, most sea rescue operations are the result of refugees calling for help on smartphones.

In their discussion of 'locative mobile social networks' or LMSNs, Adriana de Souza e Silva and Jordan Frith 'argue that what we are perhaps seeing [...] is a shift in the current model of surveillance: no longer the traditional top-down surveillance [...] but rather a model of co-surveillance in which all individuals in the network know the position of all others' (2010, 496). Of course, the uses to which mobile connectivity may be put clearly differentiates the powerful actors in a network from the non-powerful. Mobile devices enable data harvesting and the tracking of refugee movements by states or corporations, depending on which apps are in use and on access permitted by law. In Germany, legislation was drafted by the Interior Ministry in 2017 allowing the Federal Office for Migration and Refugees to access the mobile phone data of asylum seekers whose identities are difficult to evidence, 'for better enforcement of the obligation to leave' ('Interior Ministry' 2017; 'Bamf soll Identität' 2017).

And so, very quickly, we are back in the domain of enforcement, of coercion and, ultimately, of war. Cinema has long negotiated the relationship between art and war. Attempting to understand late twentieth century cinema as an instrument for 'grasping our new being-in-the-world' (Jameson 1992, 3), Fredric Jameson theorised a 'geopolitical unconscious' (1992, 3), which was underpinned by the idea 'that all thinking today is *also*, whatever else it is, an attempt to think the world system as such' (1992, 4). Jameson points to the problem of representation in this context, where 'the mode of production itself [...] whose mechanisms and dynamics are not visible [... and] cannot be detected on the surfaces scanned by satellites' create 'a fundamental representational problem [...] of a historically new and original type' (1992, 2). Others, such as Paul Virilio, have written extensively on the continuity between war and the visual, highlighting the military origins of much image-making technology. Today, we are accustomed to the overlapping of military engagement and entertainment as twin visual fields. The US military releases videos of strikes via Central Command's YouTube-hosted PR channel, CENTCOM, which has had more than 14 million views. As Judith Butler argues in the context of war photography and the frame, 'the state works on the field of perception and, more generally, the field of representability, in order to control affect' (2009, 72). This is, she writes, 'where state power exercises its forcible dramaturgy' (2009, 73). CENTCOM transmits a dramaturgy of carefully-calibrated, righteous, and not least, *visual* war.

The language of movies and games seeps into accounts of 'real' war by its very agents; in a video posted on YouTube showing excerpts from Mosse's interviews with members of the US military, a man talks of the 'exhilarating' parts of his job of bombing targets; another describes the 'satisfaction' of the mission, saying, 'our guys are excited to drop weapons' ('Bombing Isis' 2015). In a section from this video, part of which appears in *Incoming*, the hand of an Aircraft Handling Officer arranges scale models of the aircraft carrier's 70 jets on a flat board, which the crew call the 'ouija board' (Mosse 2017). The warm hand glows white and is reflected in the Perspex board, a synecdoche of the military object, gleaming like a gamer's flat screen.

What does Mosse's use of military visual technology add to this hyper-visual domain? I want to suggest that the answer lies in his close attention to what binds the biological and the technological. Mosse talks of how the 'unfamiliar and alienating technology' of the camera (quoted in Seymour 2017), even when used compassionately, 'strips the individuality from the person, turns them into a biological trace … almost like a creature' (*Incoming*: The Thing About' 2017). Certainly, the ideological freight of the camera's destructive capacity seeps into *Incoming* – deliberately so – but to me, the registering of bodies through their temperature gradients doesn't mean that people appear more or less 'human', but rather, that our modes of perception of the human are defamiliarised or estranged. There is a shift that occurs in the way we register biological life (and death). Because temperature differentials are constantly changing, depending on time of day or night and the ambient heat, and because Mosse flips the images (i.e. sometimes white is relative heat, and sometimes it is relative cold), the viewer has to do cognitive work to read the images, thinking, 'there's the hottest part, there's the coldest'. It demands deep looking.

In this way, common questions about 'humanisation' in refugee representation seem inadequate, rooted as they are in humanist notions of identification with others. In place of such identification, Mosse's camera offers a field of images of contact, residue, transfer and exchange – bodies that exist within a system in which nothing is materially bordered. The thermographic camera doesn't privilege surface. Instead, it shows up a dynamic interplay between surface, subsurface and core: we recognise the white glow of perspiration in a boy's armpit as he plays in a refugee camp as surface cooling, and the white heat of a child's skull, beneath tangled, wet hair following a sea rescue, to be the body prioritising energy for the brain.

Art that engages with technology designed for warfare is not new; nor are questions about the human limits of, and non-human extensions to, faculties of vision. In recent years, a number of drone-inspired exhibitions have responded to the forms of perspective that drone technology permits. In 2013, artist Adam Harvey, collaborating with designer Johanna Bloomfield, presented a line of 'Stealth Wear', items made 'with silver-plated fabric that reflects thermal radiation, enabling the wearer to avert overhead thermal surveillance' ('Stealth Wear' 2012). The clothing was marketed for a time at London's Privacy Gift Shop and at New York's New Museum gift shop (Pechman 2013). For Harvey, the aim of the clothing is to examine 'aesthetics of privacy and the potential for fashion to challenge authoritarian surveillance technologies' ('Stealth Wear' 2012). How might we think through an aesthetics of privacy, and the question of photographic intimacy, in the context of *Incoming*? There are several ways of approaching this question, but perhaps the most important aspect concerns the nature of the subject–spectator dynamic that is constructed. When we know that Mosse's camera can take images from 30.3 kilometres away, the aesthetic sense of closeness generated by the video installation is clearly double-edged. While many of the work's images were taken with consent and in the context of time spent with subjects, others exploit the long-range capabilities of the camera to construct close-ups of private moments. Mosse readily acknowledges the 'stolen intimacy' of some of his images (quoted in Seymour 2017).

In a sequence that has been widely reproduced in reviews and articles on *Incoming*, an Islamic wudu (cleansing) ritual is undertaken, alone, by a migrant at a truck stop in the Sahara Desert, Northern Niger (a route directly linked with climate-propelled migration). The camera frames the man front on, in a full body shot, projected enormously onto the installation's middle screen. He stands for a few moments, clearly exhausted, and then carefully kneels on the concrete. One of the fingers of his right hand moves in a small rhythmic fashion, perhaps in time to an internally voiced prayer. The man wipes his face with water from a bottle, the liquid rendered bright white before it warms to match his skin temperature and turns to black. On his website, Mosse describes the man as 'lost in prayer' – an ironic description in the context of capture on camera – adding that the sequence 'was filmed in total darkness, the man remained unaware of the camera's presence' (Mosse 2017). In an essay on *Incoming* that identifies an unwitting convergence of heat and racial metaphors in the work, Niall Martin argues that 'Mosse fuses a metaphysical discourse of the soul with the racialized optics of biopower: he makes soul an affair of skin' (Martin 2019, 14). For Martin, the implications of this fusion speak directly to questions about looking and being watched: 'we witness the convergence of a hypermodern surveillance technology with the far more archaic perspective that both Islam and the Judeo-Christian religions reserve for the eyes of angels' (2019, 1). The linking of religious and technologised notions of surveillance inevitably emphasises the power and authority embedded in Mosse's practice.

In such a context, to think about a 'relationship' between camera and subject in any practical sense is meaningless, and that poses profound ethical dilemmas for the work. *Incoming* is different from Mosse's earlier project in Congo (using a photosynthesis-sensing camera), which engendered heighted performances of macho self from its militia subjects. If the wudu sequence in *Incoming* is startling in its presentation of an *aesthetic* of intimacy, what kind of intimacy are we talking about? Is the man entitled to privacy in a public space? Is this a violation and, if so, what kind of consumption is performed by the viewer (or voyeur) of the installation? If the sequence penetrates the man's psychological interiority – which I contend it does – what does this mean for a relation of reciprocity between photographer and subject, and for the self-possession of subjects? Mosse is aware of the ambiguity of the aesthetic relation he is constructing in *Incoming*, referring in one interview to the 'invasive gaze' of the camera. Certainly, he seems to broadly share Susan

Sontag's view of the 'aggression implicit in every use of the camera' (Sontag [1977] 2008, 7); elsewhere he describes the 'self-loathing' that accompanies photographic practice, something he regards as contiguous with the issues that documentary makers face: 'there's something predatory about the camera lens. I can't escape photography but, whichever way you look at it, documentary photography is as constructed a way of seeing the world as anything else' (quoted in Seymour 2017). Not coincidentally, 'predatory' is a word that Sontag also uses (Sontag [1977] 2008, 14).

In an essay that sets out to 'critique simplistic notions of privacy as a basic human right and develop a more rigorous understanding of the culturally and historically specific character of privacy' (Miles 2015, 273), Melissa Miles observes that 'restrictions on photography in public space seem to signal larger shifts in our sense of shared public life in an era of privatization' (2015, 272). Miles insists on the need to situate concepts of privacy as a by-product of modernity, which cannot be divorced from the rise of individualism and capitalism. But in the context of many (though not all) of Mosse's refugee and migrant subjects, exclusion from the privileges of global capitalisation, vulnerability to capture by border surveillance technologies, not to mention vulnerability to climate change, mean that the question of privacy is not one that can be readily situated within a paradigm of individualism. For this reason, a sense that Mosse's images might be unethical is woven with deeper anxieties about the dismantling of full personhood consequent upon becoming a refugee.

This brings us to the heart of why Mosse's *Incoming* is so disquieting. It prompts reflection on how artistic and ethical priorities might need to shift if the arts are to play a role in a wider and deeper cultural comprehension – intellectual and emotional – of refugee crises, military violence and anthropogenic climate change. Part of why *Incoming* is troubling and aesthetically provocative is that it suggests that *making sense of the system might be a higher priority than making sense of the individual*. A refugee's thermodynamic heat signature is traceable and readable in the same way that a satellite-routed missile's trajectory is, and the violence of the latter is implicated in the forced movements of the former.

The challenge of representing the entangled hyperobjects (to return to Timothy Morton's terminology) – these being: first, our warming planet's sensitivity to climactic disturbance; second, the military-industrial / entertainment complex; and third, the effect of both on already-precarious lives – is precisely due to the hyperobject's massive 'distribut[tion] in time and space relative to humans'. It is by envisioning heat exchanges on alternately large and small scales that Mosse is able to open up a space for seeing tiny causes and effects within vastness. Ultimately, *Incoming* invites us to perceive human lives as embedded within strained, dysfunctional or destructive systems. These are systems that produce excessive waste, both hi-tech and quotidian. Wide-angle images scan a coastline at Lesvos where refugees have come ashore, and it's littered with the detritus of arrival: life vests, rubber tubes and other discarded items. The coastal border is fringed by trash. The Jungle at Calais is laid waste, the flames that engulf it mirroring the jet fighters that set out on their bombing runs. Waste emerges as the residue of sophisticated military technologies. In a video recording of Mosse's interview footage taken from the aircraft carrier, a US Navy Commanding Officer tallies up with awe the more than 10 million gallons of fuel they've 'burned through' on that particular deployment and the more than 700,000 pounds of ordnance used.

In her ecocritical discussion of literary texts that span 'all four centuries of the Anthropocene' (Sullivan 2014, 84), Heather Sullivan develops the concept of 'dirty traffic', something she perceives as a 'deterritorialised [...] global category' (2014, 85). She writes, 'The term "dirty traffic" [...] includes all [...] types of material, bodily, ecological, and cultural flows' (2014, 84). Prominent in the literary works Sullivan studies are, she notes, 'anxieties about the control of, and access to, resources; about the disruptive flows of people in the wake of wars, disasters, and changing social conditions' (2014, 84). Sullivan's move to conceptualise 'dirt' in this totalising way, enmeshing the cultural, biological and mechanical, positions the concept as akin to Morton's notion of the dispersed hyperobject. Perhaps in contrast to Morton's object philosophy, Sullivan highlights the matter of traffic (a loaded word choice): as she notes, 'Pollution has no place but rather is everyplace, and functions like a form of "dirty traffic" [...] entering virtually every organic body and cycle occurring in the biosphere (water, carbon, nitrogen, energy, etc.)' (2014, 83). What Sullivan describes is the miniscule or trace sign – i.e. toxin levels in a bloodstream – being bound with the spectacularised visual sign – i.e. the fleeing refugee. The purchase of this way of thinking, for me, lies in its offering of a framework for addressing refugee crises that doesn't see forced human movement – or traffic – in terms of (a) state borders and territories, and (b) human cartographies of legality and illegality. In this, Sullivan offers a way of thinking about artistic work similarly concerned to find new ways of thinking about refugee crises.

In a fundamental way, *Incoming* is a work that renders biological and technological systems as interlocked. Mosse's images prompt metaphorical and political reckonings at the same time as they 'see' the contours of aliveness and death within a thermodynamic system – which, as we know, tends anyway toward disorder or entropy. But in *Incoming* we are asked to witness how inevitable entropic decline might be being hastened. The images that comprise *Incoming* suggest a system that is operating at its limit, that disorder is being accelerated: death in this vision is untimely and *en masse*; ten million gallons of fuel are burned in a single military deployment; fire rages through a refugee camp; people pile onto vehicles that cross the scorching Sahara and then into boats, before they are dragged, hypothermic, from the sea. For Mosse, this tendency to disorder lends *Incoming* its metaphorical resonance as a study of how heat is akin to attention; as he puts it, 'Light is visible heat. Light fades. Heat grows cold. People's attention drifts. Media attention dwindles. Compassion is eventually exhausted. How do we find a way, as photographers and as storytellers, to continue to shed light on the refugee crisis, and to keep the heat on these urgent narratives of human displacement?' (Mosse 2017). The dilemma of attention pertains too to the wider symptomology of system dysfunction that *Incoming* shows us. The work seems to offer a prognosis of unremitting 'incoming' – of bodies, missiles, boats, trucks, objects and infrastructures – whose thermal exchanges, when imaged, construct a vision of global disturbance: polluted oceans, afflicted flesh. It is, perhaps, in this way that a camera technology originated to aid destruction might harness aesthetics for prognostic ends.

Note

1 This discussion of *Incoming* is based upon the author's viewing of the installation at the Curve Gallery, Barbican, London, on 21 April 2017.

Works cited

Agamben, Giorgio. 1998. *Homo Sacer: Sovereign Power and Bare Life*. Trans. Daniel Heller-Roazen. Stanford: Stanford University Press.

Ang, Ien. 2001. *On Not Speaking Chinese: Living Between Asia and the West*. London and New York: Routledge.

Bal, Mieke. 2007. 'Lost in Space, Lost in the Library', in *Essays in Migratory Aesthetics: Cultural Practices Between Migration and Art-making*, edited by Sam Durrant and Catherine M. Lord. Amsterdam and New York: Rodopi. 23–36.

Bal, Mieke. 2015. 'In Your Face: Migratory Aesthetics', in *The Culture of Migration: Politics, Aesthetics and Histories*, edited by Sten Pultz Moslund, Anne Ring Petersen and Moritz Schramm. London: I.B. Tauris. 147–169.

Bal, Mieke, and Miguel Hernández-Navarro, eds. 2007. *2 Move: Double Movement, Migratory Aesthetics*. Murcia: Bancaja, Eikhuizen: Zuiderzeemuseum.

'Bamf soll Identität von Asylbewerbern durch Blick ins Handy überprüfen'. 2017. *Süddeutsche Zeitung*, 19 February. Available online at: http://www.sueddeutsche.de/politik/abschiebepraxis-bamf-soll-identitaet-von-asylbewerbern-durch-blick-ins-handy-ueberpruefen-1.3385870.

Bilimoria, Purushottama. 2015. 'Transglobalism of Hindus and Sikhs in Australia', in *The Indian Diaspora: Hindus and Sikhs in Australia,* edited by Purushottama Bilimoria, Jayant Bhalchandra Bapat and Philip Hughes. New Delhi: DK Printworld. 1–34.

'Bombing Isis: on board a US floating fortress (Richard Mosse)'. 2015. Channel 4 News via YouTube, 1 October. Available online at: https://www.youtube.com/watch?v=1k Zw5MAeg2k.

Burvill, Tom. 2008. '"Politics Begins as Ethics": Levinasian Ethics and Australian Performance Concerning Refugees.' *Research in Drama Education: The Journal of Applied Theatre and Performance* 13.2: 233–244.

Butler, Judith. 2009. *Frames of War: When is Life Grievable?* London and New York: Verso.

Caldwell, Luke, and Timothy Lenoir. 2017. *The Military-Entertainment Complex.* Cambridge, MA: Harvard UP.

Castles, Stephen, and Mark Miller. [1993] 2009. *The Age of Migration: International Population Movements in the Modern World.* 4th Edition. Basingstoke: Palgrave Macmillan.

Chaudhuri, Una, and Shonni Enelow. 2014. *Research Theatre, Climate Change, and the Ecocide Project: A Casebook.* Houndmills, Basingstoke: Palgrave.

Cox, Emma. 2015. *Performing Noncitizenship: Asylum Seekers in Australian Theatre, Film and Activism.* London: Anthem Press.

Cox, Emma, and Caroline Wake. 2018. 'Envisioning Asylum/ Engendering Crisis: or, Performance and Forced Migration 10 years on.' *Research in Drama Education: The Journal of Applied Theatre and Performance* 23.2: 137–147.

Department of Foreign Affairs and Trade. 2018. *An India Economic Strategy to 2035,* Canberra: Australian Government. Available online at: https://www.dfat.gov.au/geo/india/ies/ pdf/dfat-an-india-economic-strategy-to-2035.pdf.

De Souza e Silva, Adriana, and Jordan Frith. 2010. 'Locative Mobile Social Networks: Mapping Communication and Location in Urban Spaces', *Mobilities* 5.4: 485–505.

Diversity Arts Australia, BYP Group and Western Sydney University. 2019. 'Shifting the Balance: Cultural Diversity in Leadership within the Australian Arts, Screen and Creative Sectors', Sydney: Diversity Arts Australia. Available online at: http://diversityarts.org.au/tools-resources/launch-report-culturally-diverse-arts-leadership/ (accessed 20 May 2020).

Foroutan, Naika, Coşkun Canan, Benjamin Schwarze, Steffen Beigang, and Dorina Kalkum. 2015. *Deutschland postmigrantisch II. Einstellungen von Jugendlichen und jungen Erwachsenen zu Gesellschaft, Religion und Identität.* Zweite aktualisierte Auflage. Berlin: Berliner Institut für empirische Integrations- und Migrationsforschung, Humboldt-Universität zu Berlin.

Hirsch, Marianne. 2008. 'The Generation of Postmemory', *Poetics Today* 29.1: 103–128.

'Incoming: The Thing About'. 2017. The Thing About via YouTube, 22 February. Available online at: https://www.youtube.com/watch?v=wTWnUmY2yR0.

'Interior Ministry wants unidentified refugees to give up cell phone data'. 2017. *DPA / The Local*, 20 February. Available online at: https://www.thelocal.de/20170220/interior-ministry-wants-unidentified-refugees-to-hand-over-cell-phone-data.

'Is Your Perception of Refugees Hostile?' 2017. Canvas via YouTube, 28 February. Available online at: https://www.youtube.com/watch?v=z6ps1WksU3o.

Jameson, Fredric. 1992. *The Geopolitical Aesthetic: Cinema and Space in the World System.* Bloomington and Indianapolis: Indiana University Press.

Love, Harold. 1985. 'Chinese Theatre on the Victorian Goldfields, 1858–1870.' *Australasian Drama Studies* 3.2: 47–88.

Martin, Niall. 2018. 'As "Index and Metaphor": Migration and the Thermal Imaginary in Richard Mosse's Incoming', *Culture Machine* 17: 1–19.

Mignolo, Walter. 2007. 'Delinking: The rhetoric of Modernity, the Logic of Coloniality and the Grammar of De-coloniality.' *Cultural Studies* 21.2–3: 449–514.

Mignolo, Walter. 2011. *The Darker Side of Western Modernity: Global Futures, Decolonial Options*. Durham: Duke University Press.

Mignolo, Walter, and Rolando Vázquez. 2013. 'Decolonial AestheSis: Colonial Wounds/Decolonial Healings'. *Social Text – Periscope: Decolonial AestheSis*. Available online at: http://socialtextjournal.org/periscope_topic/decolonial_aesthesis/ (accessed 25 March 2018).

Miles, Melissa. 2015. 'Photography, Privacy and the Public', *Law, Culture and the Humanities* 11.2: 270–293.

Morton, Timothy. 2013. *Hyperobjects: Philosophy and Ecology After the End of the World*. Minneapolis: University of Minnesota Press.

Mosse, Richard. 2017. Projects: *Incoming*. Available online at: http://www.richardmosse.com/projects/incoming (accessed 18 May 2020).

Ong, Aihwa. 1999. *Flexible Citizenship: The Cultural Logics of Transnationality*. Durham: Duke University Press.

Pechman, Alexandra. 2013. 'The Art World's Game of Drones', *Art News*, 23 December. Available online at: https://www.artnews.com/art-news/news/drones-as-art-2343/.

Petersen, Anne Ring. 2017. *Migration Into Art: Transcultural Identities and Art-making in a Globalised World*. Manchester: Manchester University Press.

Petersen, Anne Ring, and Moritz Schramm. 2017. '(Post-) Migration in the Age of Globalisation: New Challenges to Imagination and Representation.' *Journal of Aesthetics & Culture*, Special Issue '(Post-)Migration in the Age of Globalisation: New Challenges to Imagination and Representation' 9.2: 1–12.

Phillips, Janet, and Joanne Simon-Davies. 2017. 'Table 3: Net Overseas Migration (NOM) Since 1901' in 'Migration to Australia: A Quick Guide to the Statistics.' Parliament of Australia, 18 January. Available online at: https://www.aph.gov.au/About_Parliament/Parliamentary_Departments/Parliamentary_Library/pubs/rp/rp1617/Quick_Guides/MigrationStatistics#_Table_1:_Permanent (accessed 20 May 2020).

Quaedvlieg, Roman. 2018. 'Pacific Solution has become a mess for Coalition and a point of division for Labor', *Sydney Morning Herald*, 24 May.

'Richard Mosse's *Incoming*: Military Grade Cameras Capture the Refugee Crisis'. 2017. Canvas via YouTube, 22 February. Available online at: https://www.youtube.com/watch?v=p0IUuYjdrOU.

Schramm, Moritz. 2015. '"Home is Where the Struggle Is"': Migration, Form and Politics', in *The Culture of Migration: Politics, Aesthetics and Histories*, edited by Sten Pultz Moslund, Anne Ring Petersen and Moritz Schramm. London and New York: I.B. Tauris. 87–104.

Schramm, Moritz, Sten Pultz Moslund, and Anne Ring Petersen, eds. 2019. *Reframing Migration, Diversity and the Arts: The Postmigrant Condition*. New York and London: Routledge.

Seymour, Tom. 'Richard Mosse – Incoming'. 2017. *British Journal of Photography*, 15 February. Available online at: https://www.1854.photography/2017/02/mosse/.

Sharpe, Christina. 2016. *In the Wake: On Blackness and Being*. Durham, NC: Duke University Press.

Simon-Davies, Joanne. 2018. 'Population and migration statistics in Australia.' Parliament of Australia, 7 December. Available online at: https://www.aph.gov.au/About_Parliament/Parliamentary_Departments/Parliamentary_Library/pubs/rp/rp1819/Quick_Guides/PopulationStatistics (accessed 20 May 2020).

Sontag, Susan. [1977] 2008. *On Photography*. London: Penguin.

Spinks, Harriet. 2018. 'Boat "turnbacks" in Australia: a quick guide to the statistics since 2001.' Parliament of Australia, 20 July. Available online at: https://www.aph.gov.au/About_Parliament/Parliamentary_Departments/Parliamentary_Library/pubs/rp/rp1819/Quick_Guides/BoatTurnbacksSince2001#Table_2.

'Stealth Wear: Anti-Drone Fashion'. 2012. AH Projects, 3 December. Available online at: https://ahprojects.com/stealth-wear/.

Stewart, Lizzie. 2017. 'Postmigrant Theatre: The Ballhaus Naunynstraße Takes on Sexual Nationalism.' *Journal of Aesthetics & Culture,* themed issue: '(Post-)migration in the Age of Globalisation: New Challenges to Imagination and Representation' 9.5: 56–68.

Sullivan, Heather I. 2014. 'Dirty traffic and the dark pastoral in the Anthropocene: Narrating refugees, deforestation, radiation, and melting ice.' *Literatur für Leser* 14: 83–97.

UN (United Nations). 2017. *International Migration Report 2017: Highlights.* New York: United Nations.

Wake, Caroline. 2019. 'Theatre of the Real with Resettled Refugees: Old problems and New Solutions in The Baulkham Hills African Ladies Troupe.' *Performance Research,* 24.8: 20–30.